The
Information
Society

The Information Society

A study of continuity and change

FIFTH EDITION

John Feather

facet publishing

© John Feather 1994, 1998, 2000, 2004, 2008

Published by
Facet Publishing
7 Ridgmount Street
London WC1E 7AE
www.facetpublishing.co.uk

Facet Publishing is wholly owned by CILIP: the Chartered Institute of Library
and Information Professionals.

First published by Library Association Publishing 1994
Second edition 1998
Third edition 2000
Fourth edition 2004 by Facet Publishing
This fifth edition 2008

British Library Cataloguing in Publication Data
A catalogue record for this book is available from the British Library.
ISBN 978-1-85604-636-7

Typeset in 10.5/15pt University Old Style and Zurich by Facet Publishing.
Printed and made in Great Britain by MPG Books Ltd, Bodmin, Cornwall.

Contents

Contents

Preface to the fifth edition

The first edition of this book was written and published in 1994, and a second revised edition appeared in 1998. Two years later, there was a third edition at the beginning of a new century, once again taking account of new developments and rapid change. The revision of the fourth edition took this process further. It is a measure of the continuing pace of change that this further revised edition is now needed, and that it was necessary to make changes which were significant, and in some instances extensive. Although *The Information Society* was not, in the conventional sense, a textbook, I know that it has been widely used by students, especially those on courses in information studies, librarianship and communications studies in which a broad understanding of the nature of the information society is an essential underpinning of more advanced work. That was its intended audience, although I always hoped that it would be of wider interest as well.

The original aim of the book remains unchanged. The fundamental argument and structure remain intact. They grew out of the belief that we cannot understand the so-called 'information society', which has brought us into the 21st century, unless we have some understanding of how information has been accumulated, analysed and disseminated in the past. We have to distinguish between comparatively superficial changes, which are merely technical, and the great shifts in the paradigm of human communications that have taken place three times in the history of mankind. The third of those shifts has been argued to have created – and still to be creating – the information society. The pace of change is unprecedented; the world wide web, which is central to much of what is discussed here, was barely mentioned in the first edition, but was the dominant format of the internet by the time that the second edition was prepared. It is now already the subject of historical studies, autobiographical reminiscence and indeed a new mythology. The internet itself is one of the key loci of the paradigm shift, although its growth will soon peak: if the present rate of increase in users were sustained, the number of users would exceed the total population of the world in less than a decade!

Perhaps the most radical change in the 14 years since the first edition was published has been that so much of what was then described in some detail (such as e-mail) is now part of everyday life and needs no description. Indeed, in preparing the fourth edition, I was able to assume that readers had a general familiarity with many of the tools and systems that I was discussing. The world wide web is the first port of call for almost anyone under the age of 30 seeking information, and for many who are older – in some cases far older! – than that. Mobile phones are an essential part of life. Digital television transmitted by satellite has not only revolutionized home entertainment, but also industries as diverse as film-making and sports promotion. Whole areas of economic activity are being transformed by the technologies of the information society, from the complaints services of airlines (now as likely to be in Bangalore as in Birmingham or Baltimore) to the music industry (assaulted, perhaps fatally, by digital copying and transmission).

We are now familiar with the concept of the 'Google generation', people born since about 1990 who cannot remember a world in which Google did not exist. They will begin to enter higher education during the lifetime of the present edition of this book. That fact alone makes it all the more important to understand that what is offered here is a study of continuity as well as change. The starting-point is the past, and briefly the very remote past, for which I make no apology. Although much of this book is concerned with the implications of technologies that are still in a dynamic, and perhaps early, stage of development, the social and intellectual assumptions, customs and practices on which they are impacting is very old. Computers and computer networks are only the latest expression of the fundamental human desire to record and to communicate information. It is only in this longer historical perspective that we can begin to understand both the enormity and the limitations of what is happening now and what we are trying to do. In this context, I have attempted to examine some of the traditional systems of information provision - by publishers and by authors - as well as by librarians, and to suggest ways in which they are being challenged and modified by the use of information technology.

It is, however, central to my view of the information society that the changes that we are now experiencing cannot simply be characterized as developments in computing, even though computing is arguably the principal driver of change and certainly provides the key tool in many of the changes and developments in information management in the last two decades. But there is a wider context, some of it much wider than the scope of this book. Despite all the changes (including some in my own position on, and understanding of, some of the issues involved), I can still endorse some words that I wrote in the preface to the first edition in 1994, for most of us the last year of the world before the web:

> The flow of information in society runs through many channels, of which the most common, and in some ways the most significant, are the mass media. Broadcasting, in particular, appears regularly in this book as an integral part of society's information infrastructure. The underlying argument, which runs throughout this book, is that new systems of information storage and communication have supplemented rather than supplanted what existed before. Just as we still use handwriting, despite the existence of so many mechanical substitutes for it (printing, typewriting, word-processing, and so on), so we shall continue to use the printed word even though many other media are available to us. We read newspapers despite the ubiquity of television. The diversity of media gives us greater power to communicate in the most effective way once we learn how to exploit it.
>
> It is in this context that I have tried to suggest some of the issues that arise out of the problem of gaining access to the information which we can so ingeniously and efficiently store and disseminate. I have explored the benefits of the information revolution, as well as some of its consequences for those who are disadvantaged and disempowered by technological change. I have also suggested some of the political consequences of how we store and process information: how information systems can be abused as easily as they can be used. Finally, I have brought this back to the context of the provision of information through institutions and by those with professional skills in the management of both.

I hope that I have raised as many questions as I have answered; indeed, some of the questions admit of no answer. At a time of such rapid technological development, social evolution and political change, it is difficult to be certain of the present and impossible to make confident predictions about the future.

I hope, however, that at least some of what I have written here addresses issues that are of longer-term significance than today's management theory or tomorrow's technological miracle which will be forgotten next year. In essence, this book, like the lectures of which it is a remote derivative, is intended to provoke thought rather than merely to convey fact.

Finally, I should like to thank all of those who have – often without knowing it – contributed to this book. They include at least a dozen cohorts of students, and many colleagues and friends throughout the world. My special thanks, however, are due to James Dearnley who falls into all three categories, and both helps me and forces me to keep up to date!

John Feather

Introduction

The information society: myth and reality

As we approach the end of the first decade of the new century, people over the age of 35 in the industrialized countries are increasingly conscious of living in a world that is profoundly and fundamentally different from that into which many of them were born. In less than two decades, we have seen technological, economic, political and cultural change on a scale which, as a retrospective view becomes possible, is beginning to justify the use of the word 'revolution' to describe it. But revolution is a word that we associate with violence, with the storming of the Bastille or the bombardment of the Winter Palace. The 1990s were indeed a violent decade in some places, but our revolution was only indirectly a part of that. It began in the 1970s and is not yet complete; it has been at once less obvious and more far-reaching than a mere change in a regime or even in a whole political system. It has been a revolution in our way of living, which, in one way or another, has affected every human being on the planet.

The symbol of the revolution is the computer, the 'electronic brain' of the 'boffins' in science fiction films of two generations ago, which now seem far older than their 40 or 50 years. The computer is in every office, on most desks and in millions of homes. Behind the scenes it is involved in almost everything we do, from buying our groceries to making a telephone call. Even after more than a century of almost continuous innovation in the technology of communication, and the invention of devices from the telegraph and the telephone to the television, the computer is perceived, however vaguely, as being in some way different. By understanding that difference, we can begin to understand the new society which the computer is helping to create, the revolution which it has both inspired and driven.

It is now two centuries since the last comparable revolution was at its height in Britain. The exploitation of the power of steam was creating a new economy, and in so doing reordering patterns of work, social relationships and the structure and political organization of society. The new arrangements which stabilized in the first half of the 19th century were recognizably the successor of what had gone before, but unmistakably different from it. Institutions that survived were changed; many vanished, and many new ones were created. The revolution through which we are now living is at least as great in its significance.

The steam engine was the motive power, both literal and metaphorical, of the industrial revolution; the computer is driving the revolution which is taking us into the third millennium. Why has this machine become so important? What is so special about these devices that has made them the force behind changes far greater than those wrought by any other invention of an inventive century? The answer lies in their ability to simulate skills and attributes that we once thought were unique to ourselves: memory, logic, communication. Machines that are able to emulate, and in some ways to surpass, the intellectual and social capacities of those who make them are both fascinating and frightening. The virtually unlimited production and availability of such devices cannot leave any aspect of human thought and activity wholly untouched.

Communication and memory are central to the human experience. So far as we know, we are the only creatures on earth with a true sense of history, a desire and an ability to remember and analyse events in the past, and to make arrangements that allow us to record our knowledge and ideas in perpetuity, so that they can be recovered and understood by generations not yet born in societies which do not yet exist. Uniquely, we can communicate across time and space and have developed systems and devices that enable us to do so. These developments began in the dawn of human history, with the evolution of language itself (which some anthropologists would argue is the dawn of human history in any meaningful sense) and the later invention of the first systems for recording and preserving language in a material form.

The information-dependent society that is emerging from our revolution

- the post-industrial revolution as some analysts call it - combines both profound change and fundamental continuity. It can only be understood in context. Part of this context is historical: the development of writing, printing and systems of communication. Part of it is economic: the means by which systems for the communication of information have become enmeshed in general systems of social and economic organization, so that information and the means of its storage and transmission have been commodified. A third part is political: commodified information is valorized by more than merely the cost of its production and distribution, for there is a real power to be derived from its possession and a loss of empowerment caused by its absence. These hypotheses about the origins, development and implications of the information society are at the heart of this book.

We begin with an historical survey, which sweeps without apology across much of the history of mankind. In that history, we observe first the development of writing, as people seek to preserve more information than their memories can hold and communicate it to those to whom they cannot speak. We trace the development of different systems of writing until one - the alphabet - emerges and supersedes almost all of the others because it is an adaptable and flexible means of preserving the languages in which we think and speak. Even the alphabet, however, cannot cope with all the concepts that the human mind can invent. Systems were developed which enabled our ancestors to record sound (as musical notation), numeric data and the relationship between them (as numbers and symbols for mathematical functions) and visual representation of size, shape and colour.

In the second phase of our history, a mechanical device - printing - was applied to the chronicling and dissemination of the information which was thus recorded. The invention of printing has been seen as a defining moment in the history of mankind. Certainly, it facilitated important changes in the organization and structure of western European culture, religion and politics, and was to be one of the instruments of European domination of almost all of the rest of the world. In the smaller world of communications, printing had another effect which we consider at length: it was the fundamental reason for the commodification of communications. A printer, we shall argue, needed more than merely skills in order to practise his craft successfully; a printer also needed both capital for the equipment with which the product was made and distribution systems through which the product could be sold. The printed book was the first mass medium, because it was economically impossible for it to be anything else.

Out of printing there developed the vast edifice of the publishing industry, the first significant manifestation of communications entering the world of commerce. The process of writing, producing and selling printed books was, for 400 years, the unchallenged system of communication between literate people. It became so familiar as to become a paradigm; its vocabulary and some of its customs have been imitated by the producers and consumers of very different media. In this book, the paradigm has been exploited to the full. There is a substantial analysis of the process of book publishing, and of the industry that has developed around it. This is developed as a model of commercial systems for the communication of knowledge and information, which can be applied in turn to the other media that have proliferated in the last 100 years.

The development of those other media – sound, vision, computing, and various combinations of them – is the final historical strand in this study. The history of information and communication in the last 150 years is, in part, the history of the development of new devices and systems which have extended our power to communicate in two ways. First, they have made it more systematic and faster and hence more efficient. Secondly, and more importantly, they have extended the scope of what can be communicated. Above all, accurate representations of visual phenomena – photography, film, video – have become a part of our daily lives. We have moved beyond text and language into the storage and communication of images of the visual world in which we actually live. Other inventions have speeded the transmission of information: the telegraph, the telephone, radio, television. These tools of communication are the building blocks of the information society. An increasingly literate society has, paradoxically, become more dependent than ever on oral and visual communication systems.

Only at the very end of our historical story do we reach the computer, and yet as soon as we do so we can begin to see its all-pervasive effects. The computer has brought together so many of the developments of the past. It has both demanded and facilitated the convergence of technologies, which allows us to combine computing with telecommunications and the digitization of text and image to permit almost instantaneous worldwide (and indeed extra-terrestrial) transmission of data.

The historical approach in Chapters 1 and 2 is essentially an attempt to sketch the history of the storage, communication and retrieval of information, in terms of media and technology. We turn next to the economic issues that have arisen, which are becoming more acute and which are being more urgently addressed because of the increasing predominance of technology in the process of information provision and the delivery of information services. Information, as has already been suggested, was commodified and valorized by the invention of printing and the consequent development of an industry which used printing as its key technology. Publishing – the paradigm – is in the front line of exposure to change under the impact of the information revolution. The market-place itself is being redefined and extended. Some activities traditionally associated with publishing and others traditionally associated with libraries are being disaggregated and recombined. The new configurations have wide implications far beyond the boundaries of the academic world in which many of them originated. E-mail and electronic publishing are only two of the more obvious applications of the combination of computing and telecommunications which we broadly describe as 'information technology'.

The printed word, which has been the traditional commodity in the information market-place, was supplemented and to a limited extent displaced throughout the 20th century. The information revolution encompasses all those media that communicate information to recipients. In the developed world, and indeed far beyond it, the most potent medium of all is television, the near-universal domestic source of information, entertainment and social interaction. Broadcasting, first in sound only and then in both sound and vision, has been with us for nearly 100 years. Its ability to transmit information and opinion instantaneously, with great apparent authority and directly to the home, was a force whose power was recognized before World War II and has been consistently exploited by governments, pressure groups and commercial interests ever since it was identified. Radio and television are integral to the information revolution, and yet they are also subject to it. Satellite broadcasting, which is computer-dependent, has brought a new sense of freedom to the television industry, but, like so many other developments, has also reiterated, if reiteration were needed, the need for huge capital investment to gain access to this key medium of information and influence.

It is not only the mass media that have changed the information marketplace. Broadcasting is, by definition, a public activity. Information, however, is increasingly seen, in some respects, as being too valuable to be public. Stored in databases throughout the world is information with commercial potential to which access is restricted by the ability of the information-seeker to pay for it. Again a revolution is being wrought. The library is the historic paradigm of information storage and retrieval as publishing is of information marketing. Libraries, like publishers, have been in the front line of change. These changes are far from superficial; it is not just that libraries now contain a wide range of media, and are increasingly dependent upon technology both for their management and for the provision of services to users. There are far more profound economic changes, for libraries are part of the increasingly commercialized chain of information supply. Traditionally, the library was merely the customer of the publisher. Now it has the potential to be the publisher's partner in many enterprises, and librarians are reassessing their attitudes to the cost of information supply. Outside the confines of the institutional library, information providers have few of the inhibitions that have traditionally made librarians look askance at such matters. Information has values assigned to it, and it is provided at a profit to the provider; prices are determined by the forces of the market.

It is out of these economic themes covered in Chapters 3 and 4 that the political themes that predominate in Chapters 5 and 6 emerge. On a global scale, there is a growing gap between the rich and the poor in access to information as in so much else. The technological developments of the last 60 years have made more information more available to more people than at any other time in human history. At the same time, however, the cost of those technologies, and the cost of gaining access to information through them, have made it often difficult and sometimes impossible for information to be obtained by its potential beneficiaries. This is the central paradox and the central political dilemma of the information revolution. As in the industrial revolution, in different ways, the benefits to the majority, encompassed in the abstraction of 'society', are being achieved partly at the expense of weaker and poorer individuals whose skills are becoming outmoded and whose earning power is consequently declining.

The revolution in the communication of information has created what is sometimes called a 'global village'. Yet instant access and instantaneous transmission depend upon a vastly expensive infrastructure of telecommunications and broadcasting systems on the part of the providers, and the acquisition of appropriate equipment (and sometimes skills) on the side of the consumers. Those who are excluded are the majority of the populations of most of the Third World and significant minorities even in richer countries. Even in the USA, the cabling of the 'information superhighway', the optic fibre network which can bring digital communications to the home, was politicized as the provider companies avoided poorer areas of cities to concentrate on the richer areas where demand and profits was higher. The gap between information rich and information poor is increasingly overt.

If that gap is the wider political dimension of the information revolution, its most obvious immediate political consequence has been to change, or to threaten or promise to change, the relationship between the state and its own citizens. Governments, like businesses, cannot function without information, and as they become more complex so do their information needs. Much of this is not only legitimate, it is both essential and benevolent. A modern state cannot function without such basic data as that provided by censuses, tax returns and electoral registers. There is, however, a debate, perhaps not yet sufficiently well articulated, about the boundaries of the legitimate information needs of a democratic state. Information about identifiable individuals is sensitive, and yet there are cases in which its dissemination, perhaps to a tightly defined group of recipients, is clearly in the public interest. In other cases, there can be no such interest, and dissemination is clearly an invasion of legitimate privacy. But there is an increasing number of less clear-cut areas, where the organs and agencies of the state are collecting information of great potential value or harm. The process of regulation - of balancing the general good against individual rights - has begun, but is still embryonic. The whole issue, complex enough already, was at the beginning of the 21st century further complicated by the growing concern with international networks of both criminals and terrorists; they are also among the beneficiaries of information and communications technology.

Historically, the state has always been a participant in the process of information transfer. It regulates the operation of the market-place through laws that control the dissemination of intellectual property, such as copyrights and patents, and also, in most cases, by exercising a certain level of moral jurisdiction through censorship. The state's role, however, like so much else, is being transformed by the information revolution. The very concept of copyright, which for 300 years has been the legal foundation-stone of the publishing industry, becomes blurred when the technology of copying is uncontrollably widely available. As the historic functions of publishers and libraries begin to converge in electronic publishing and electronic document supply services, the very nature of copyright will need to be redefined. There are changes too in the general perception of the state's right to intervene by intercepting private communications and controlling the content or availability of those intended for public consumption. These are lively political issues which touch on the fundamental principles of political democracy and an open society.

These three aspects of the evolution of the information society – the historical, the economic, the political – are considered in turn. Each raises its own questions, yet all are interrelated. The questions are not new, but they have all been made more urgent by the power of the computer to store, process and transmit information. In the industrialized countries it is no longer possible to conduct many of the most basic transactions of daily life without using the power of computers. Our greatest tool of information and communication is in danger of becoming our master. Much of this book is concerned with trying to define the issues that are raised by this prospect.

Finally, there is one group of people in society who have a special role to play in the information revolution. Computer scientists and information workers are the engineers of the post-industrial revolution (see Chapter 7). More than any other group, publishers, librarians and archivists have seen their professions transformed; whole new professions have come into existence as governments, businesses, industries and institutions have struggled to reposition themselves to deal with the new technologies of information and communication. In those parts of the world where the information revolution has made its greatest impact, the information professionals are becoming a larger and larger part of the workforce as a whole. But it is not only those professionals whose lives are being profoundly changed. Patterns of work and patterns of employment are being transformed as radically now as they were in the move from an agricultural to an industrial economy 200 years ago. Manufacturing itself is no longer dependent upon the mass employment of labour as computer-based devices are made which can undertake the routine work of making and assembling parts. We are living in the midst of this revolution. Those who are seeking to enter the information and communications professions – for whom this book is principally intended – need to be able to formulate the questions to which the answers will prescribe the limits of their professional lives. Some of those questions are posed, and a few of the answers are suggested, in the rest of this book.

PART 1
The historical dimension

Chapter 1

From script to print

The origins of writing

The earliest evidence for the existence of *Homo sapiens* derives from the interpretation of archaeological and palaeontological evidence rather than from records consciously made by people themselves. Our species was already in an advanced stage of physiological and intellectual development before we began to leave a deliberate mark on the world around us. The first such marks, perhaps the first consciously created records, are the graphic representations of daily life which have been found in caves in France and elsewhere. Scholars debate the significance of these, whether they are religious, social, or merely artistic; for our purposes, their importance is that we have here the first evidence of a species which sought some means to represent the world in which it lived. It found a material on which the representation could be recorded - the rock walls of a cave - and a medium - natural dyes - in which it could be made.

Between palaeolithic cave paintings and the first real records of human activities there are millennia. The earliest cave paintings are generally considered to date from 40,000 years ago; even so, they embody the basic principle of meeting a perceived need by developing, or making use of, a combination of medium and material. All subsequent systems have developed from that same perception of need.

When complex societies began to evolve in various parts of Asia, their very complexity forced them to consider, possibly even consciously, how complexity could be managed. Pictorial representation, forceful as it is and important as it continues to be, is limited. While pictures can convey shapes and colours far more effectively than words, and can often give greater clarity than a verbal description of an action or a scene, they are less effective in embodying abstractions or ideas. A picture can show the shape and colour of a house but cannot state its financial value. A picture can represent the appearance of a person, but cannot show what that person is thinking. A picture can reproduce, with great accuracy, the appearance of a car, but it can neither explain how it works nor show it in motion. To preserve an image of anything other than a purely visual and static world, we first need a system which allows us to express language in some representational form.

The essence of all writing systems, the oldest and still the most important means of achieving this, is that they allow language which describes the abstract to take on a concrete form, and in some cases can simulate the language even more accurately by representing its sounds as well as the ideas which the sounds convey. The earliest writing systems, however, were non-alphabetic, and clearly derived from the practice of drawing pictures. The history of the earliest writing is necessarily obscure, but it seems likely that it evolved in the Middle East about 5000 years ago.

Its purpose was utilitarian. A stage of societal development had been reached in which something like a state was evolving. There were rulers and ruled. There was a social and economic order in which some were richer and more powerful than others. Wealth and power depended upon many factors, of which the most important was perhaps access to the raw materials of human survival: food and water. Those who were powerful enough to control natural resources were able to exercise control over others, whether on a small or a large scale. Men fought for the control of such resources. There were organized groups, in which submitting to the leadership of the strongest or the cleverest was clearly advantageous to the less strong or the less clever if, in return, they were able to share in the resources. The gradual emergence of the concept of the state with a common ruler and common interests led to the need for common resources. It was this that seems to have forced the development of writing systems.

The monarchies of the Tigris-Euphrates valley - on the borders of modern Iran and Iraq - raised taxes from their subjects in order to sustain themselves and their actions for the common good. As this process was regularized, it became necessary to record what had been paid, for what purpose, and by and to whom payment had been made. This necessitated a system which could record quantity as well as indicate the material in which payment had been made. Thus if the ruler demanded a proportion of the crop as a form of taxation (in return for the defence of the farmer's land), the writing system had to be able to represent the crop itself, its total size, the relationship between that total and the farmer's liability, and the fact of payment having been made. No purely graphic system could achieve this, and what evolved was a means of using modified pictorial images.

Corn, the most basic commodity of such a society, was represented by a symbol clearly derived in part from its appearance. Numbers are more complicated, but even for them a form of visual representation was possible. It was based on the fingers of the human hand, so that a single stroke represented 'one', two strokes 'two', and so on. Symbols could be used which described people by their attributes: a ceremonial headdress or crown for the king, a hoe for the peasant, and so on. A representational writing system of this kind was limited but practical.

A writing system, however, can never be independent of the medium in which it can be used. Such a medium, like the writing system itself, emerges out of social necessity and environmental circumstances. In the Tigris–Euphrates valley there is water, sand and intense heat. Taken together, they allowed the peoples of the region to develop simple but effective mechanisms for turning mud into bricks by combining the sand and the water, and drying it in the sun. As it dried, inscriptions could easily be made in the surface of the brick, which, when it was baked, would be permanent. It is on such clay tablets that the earliest written records of mankind are to be found.

The system of writing used in the ancient Middle East is known to scholars as *cuneiform* (literally 'wedge-shaped', derived from the shape of the instrument used for inscribing the symbols in the clay). Significant numbers of clay tablets containing such inscriptions have been found by archaeologists, and can be seen in museums around the world. Cuneiform, however, was not unique. Other systems evolved along similar lines elsewhere, many of them, like cuneiform, essentially derived from an attempt to use a modified form of pictorial representation of objects. Such modifications, however, still carried with them the essential disadvantages of representational systems based, however distantly, on pictorial images: an inability to convey abstractions and actions. It was possible to represent a king, but less easy to illustrate 'monarchy' or 'state'. Some writing systems achieved this by using the image of an object (a crown to represent 'king') to mean the abstraction which the object itself symbolized or embodied (a crown to represent 'sovereignty'). The script which began to be developed in China in about 1500 BCE became particularly adept at this. Characters for objects could even be combined to represent a concept associated with the combination.

The transition from purely pictorial systems (*pictographs*) to systems which combined pictographs and characters for more abstract concepts (*hieroglyphs*) took place independently in China and in Egypt. Neither pictographs nor hieroglyphs, however, really address the central problem of the representation of language. Language evolved as sounds, and different languages use sounds in different ways. Some sounds, or phonemes, which are common in some languages are unknown in others; the 'th' sound in words like 'the' in English does not exist in French, and is as notoriously difficult to a native speaker of French as the French 'r' and 'u' sounds (as in '*rue*') are to native English speakers. Words used to describe objects, actions or attributes are merely commonly understood combinations of sounds. The word 'house' has no absolute meaning any more than '*maison*' has; it merely happens, through a process of development over many centuries, that these two random combinations of sound have come to signify the same object to speakers of different languages. By going behind what is signified by words to the sounds of which the words are constituted, we reach the raw material of language itself.

The realization of this, whether consciously or unconsciously, led to the next stage in the development of writing systems: the use of symbols to represent sounds. The earliest systems, known as *syllabaries*, took the phoneme, or unit of pronunciation, as their building blocks. The 'th' combination is a phoneme in English, but not in French, where the juxtaposition of the two letters is pronounced quite differently. Phonemes could only be represented symbolically, since they were derived from sounds, not objects. Syllabaries broke the link between visual represent-ation and the representation of human speech. The Chinese pictographs, for example, having been adopted by the Japanese, were modified by them and eventually replaced by a syllabary in which each symbol represents a phoneme. Thus symbols can be combined and recombined to form the visual representation of words, regardless of the meaning of the words themselves.

The alphabet

Although the syllabary could be argued to be a more advanced writing system than hieroglyphs or pictographs, it was still limited in its applications. Where phonemes vary between languages, each language needs its own character set to represent them. Only by breaking the phonemes into even more basic units can the final flexibility be achieved. It was in the Middle East, yet again, that this final stage of development took place, about 3000 years ago. The Phoenicians, a trading people living on the eastern shores of the Mediterranean, developed a form of representing speech which eliminated all pictorial images and almost all represent-ations of phonemes. The Greek alphabet derived directly from this and in that script the phonemes all but vanished. The few survivors, such as θ (theta, the English 'th' sound as in 'the'), are conspicuous by being unusual. For all practical purposes, the ancient Greeks used an alphabet just as we do. A variation of the Greek alphabet, eliminating the remaining phonemic characters, was developed by the Romans, and survives today as our 'Roman' or 'Latin' alphabet, the alphabet in which nearly all European languages are written.

The Latin alphabet is not, however, unique. Greek still survives. Moreover, it was modified by early Christian missionaries to represent some of the Slavic languages of eastern Europe, and in this form, as Cyrillic, it is in use for Russian, Ukrainian, Bulgarian, Serbian and other languages of the region. Another branch of the original Middle Eastern alphabet developed differently among the speakers of Semitic languages, and became both

Hebrew and Arabic. All these various developments have one essential feature in common: an alphabet's adaptability to different languages which have different phonemes. Thus the Latin alphabet can be used for English, French, German, and so on, with only minor modifications such as the use of accents. Cyrillic is also used for several languages. Arabic script is used for Urdu and for other languages in western Asia; a modified form of the Pali script of India is used for the quite different Thai language, and so on. Even more remarkably, languages can change from one script to another. Turkish used to be written in Arabic script, but since 1924 has been written in the Latin alphabet. In many Asian countries, transliteration of public notices, road signs, and the like are a common sight to aid the western visitor. Many of the languages of Africa and the islands of the Pacific, never reduced to writing by their native speakers, can be written only in the Latin characters introduced by colonial conquerors and missionaries. An alphabet is an almost infinitely flexible tool for the representation of language, and hence for its storage and transmission.

The survival of the Latin alphabet after the dissolution of the western half of the Roman Empire in the fifth century is one of the key events in the cultural history of Europe. It was the alphabet in which the sacred writings of the Christian Church were written in the West, as well as being a link with the fading memories of the former glories of Rome, which was still seen as a model of good government and vibrant culture. The alphabet was used when the new rulers of western Europe, the tribes of the east and the north, began to write their own languages, and thus became the alphabet of the emerging western vernaculars. Those northern languages which had evolved their own syllabaric systems, such as the runes used for Norse, rapidly succumbed. The common alphabet has preserved and embodied something of the cultural unity of the West for 1500 years, and allowed western Europeans to learn each other's languages with comparative ease. The absence of a common language has been less problematic than it might have been because of the existence of a common alphabet.

The central role of an alphabet in the storage and communication of information cannot be overstated. In essence, it permits the representation in permanent and commonly understood form of a multiplicity of languages, and hence of any concept which can be expressed in the languages which it represents. It minimizes the obstacles to understanding, is easy to learn, easy to use and readily adaptable. It is not, however, perfect.

In moving to the greater flexibility of alphabetic systems, there were losses as well as gains. The hunting scenes so vividly portrayed by the cave artists can be described in words only with great difficulty and inevitable loss of impact. Colour, sound and some actions are notoriously difficult to describe. No words can express the concept of 'red' to a sightless or colour-blind person, or the concept of 'loud' to a person with no hearing, any more than we can see 'good' or hear 'light'. Moreover, human sensory abilities vary from person to person. To those with perfect pitch, the mere words 'middle C' convey a precise sound which they can 'hear' and perhaps reproduce vocally; to others it may conjure up a visual image of a particular note on the keyboard of a piano, or of a piece of musical notation; to some, it will mean nothing at all. Both knowledge and ability limit our capacity to understand the concepts represented by alphabetic symbols made into words; there are, therefore, limits to the usefulness of the alphabetic symbols themselves.

Images, sounds and numbers

The visual representation of objects, colours and shapes has always been an integral part of human culture. As we have seen, it was the first aspect of human experience to be recorded in a permanent form, and except when representational art has been banned for cultural reasons (as in some Islamic traditions, for example) it has never ceased to exist. Visual imagery has, however, gradually extended beyond simply representing what can be seen. Map-making was perhaps the first example of this. The ancient geographers drew patterns which illustrated their understanding of the shape of geographical features, but they did so in a way which they could not possibly have seen. Until well into the 20th century, almost no human being had ever risen far enough above the surface of the earth to be able to see the shapes of coastlines, for example, or the courses of rivers. Maps have always been made by using conventions of signs and symbols to represent what is believed to exist but cannot be seen as a whole. The conventions, and the techniques behind them, have changed, but the essential principle has remained the same.

The alphabet embodies a key principle of the communication of information: the need for a means to represent language in a permanent and generally understood form. A map takes this one stage further: the communication of information by the visual representation of that which has to be deduced because it can neither be easily described in language, nor verified by visual observation. Alphabetic and visual information recording systems cannot, however, embody the whole range of human communications. Language embodies thought and speech; pictorial images, whether realistically or symbolically representational, embody what we can see; but we also hear things other than speech. Some non-speech sounds can indeed be alphabetically represented; we can describe a dog as 'barking', a word which signifies, although it does not represent, the sound which the animal makes. We can even try to represent the sound made by the dog as 'woof' or some similar attempt at an onomatopoeic word. No words, however, can convey the sounds of the wind, birdsong or music, and for the latter in particular, a whole series of systems of notation have been developed to allow composers to represent their wishes in a way that is comprehensible to performers. Musical notation, like the symbols on a map, is a recording system which acts as a surrogate for, and works similarly to, an alphabet, in a situation in which the alphabet is inadequate because language itself is inadequate.

Most difficult of all is the representation of quantitative data. Measurement was a concept which was highly developed in the very societies in which the earliest writing systems were developed, but none entirely solved the problem of the representation of numbers and of calculations in which numbers were used. The Greeks developed a vastly complicated system using alphabetic characters, as did the Romans, but even the latter's was almost impossibly clumsy for all but the most elementary mathematical applications. It was the Arabs who finally solved the problem in the ninth century CE, developing nine symbols to represent the numerals from one to nine and (crucially) adopting the Indian concept of zero, and the now universal symbols to represent the basic functions of addition, subtraction, multiplication and division. Mathematical symbols, like musical notation, are a substitute for the alphabet used to convey concepts for which language is inadequate or inappropriate.

The first media

All these various systems of representing information, whether linguistic, numeric, visual or aural, depend on the existence not only of a means of representation - a system of recording - but also of a means of preserving the representation, that is a form of recording medium. The earliest media were natural substances, such as rock, bone or wood. The rock of the cave was unmodified from its natural form unless the surface was washed or prepared in some other way before the painter set to work. Other media were, however, changed, sometimes quite significantly. Bone, for example, which is the medium on which the oldest Chinese characters are preserved, had to be cleaned and perhaps polished or planed before it could be used. Similarly, wood had to be prepared by cutting, planing and perhaps sizing. Even the 'natural' media, therefore, were actually the products of human ingenuity and skill, just like the recording systems which they were designed to carry.

The baked clay tablets of the Assyrians were to prove to be more typical than wood or bone for the future development of media. Different societies evolved different media according to their needs, their technological capacity and the availability of materials. Indeed, in many cultures different media were used for different purposes. The ancient Romans, for example, continued to use stone for monumental inscriptions (as we do ourselves) long after papyrus, vellum and parchment had become common; the choice between the last three was determined partly by purpose and partly by economic considerations. Similarly, the Egyptians painted and inscribed hieroglyphs even after they developed a syllabary that could more conveniently be written on papyrus or parchment.

The important thing about recording media is that they should be appropriate. Appropriateness is not an absolute concept, but it can be broadly defined in terms of fitness for purpose. An inscription on stone, which can be made only by a highly skilled person over a comparatively long period of time and which can be neither modified nor easily transported, is clearly quite unsuitable for some casual purpose such as making a note of domestic accounts or an *aide-mémoire* of a course of action which has been agreed. Cultures therefore evolve different media for different purposes. For most of the recording systems which we have already discussed, what was needed was a smooth surface on which symbols could be inscribed, written or painted. In turn this required some kind of implement, and (for writing and painting) a substance which could be applied to the surface. The familiar version of this is of pen, ink and paper, all of which have existed, in some form or other, for at least 4000 years.

The most useful media for writing are, literally, the most flexible. Clay tablets, polished stone, bones, wood bark and similar surfaces are solid, but clumsy. They take up a great deal of storage space, and some of them (clay and wood, for example) deteriorate rapidly or (like bone or baked clay) are easily damaged. A strong flexible surface, on the other hand, can be easily stored (by rolling or folding) and is less susceptible to damage, although far from permanent in some cases. In western Asia, in the first millennium BCE, various kinds of vegetable matter and animal derivatives were used to make such materials. The papyrus reed, which grows in the shallows along the banks of the Nile in Egypt and Sudan, could easily be processed into a reasonably good writing material. Although it was a little fragile if it was bent, it could be sewn into large sheets, and rolled for storage if it was treated carefully. The surface, when sized, would hold ink without blotting, and the raw material itself was readily available. Papyrus became one of the most common writing materials in the eastern Mediterranean towards the end of the first millennium BCE.

The alternative to vegetable matter was to use suitably processed animal skins. When stripped from the flesh of a dead beast, cleaned of its hair, and partially tanned, the hide of the cow, goat or camel could be turned into a very effective writing surface. Like papyrus, it could hold the ink, while it had the additional merit of being stronger in some respects. Vellum and parchment are less susceptible to damp than is papyrus, and can also be folded as well as rolled. This was to be of particular importance as the modern form of the book began to evolve in the first and second centuries CE.

The development of the book

The development of the familiar form of the book is a defining moment in the history of information storage and retrieval in the West, almost as significant in its way as the invention of the alphabet. Until about the beginning of the Common Era, written documents were either single sheets, stored (if at all) flat, or long scrolls of sheets of papyrus, vellum or parchment, sewn or glued together end to end. These were stored in cylindrical cases, made of wood or metal, of which examples have been found among the petrified ruins of Pompeii and Herculaneum, and which are still used for ceremonial purposes in storing the scriptures in Jewish liturgical rites.

Towards the end of the first century BCE, small sheets of parchment held together by a single thread at the corner began to be used as informal notebooks, and it was from these that the modern form of the book (the *codex*) was gradually developed over a period of about a century. A key stage in this development was when the sewing together of single sheets was replaced by the folding of the sheets before sewing, creating a codex which was at once simpler and stronger. It seems that the development of the codex was particularly associated with the Christians, perhaps because they needed portable books which could easily be concealed for their missionary activities in the Roman Empire. When Christianity became the established religion of the Empire in the early fourth century CE, the scroll came to be associated with the pagan past. The codex proved so convenient that it even triumphed as a medium for the pagan classics.

The general adoption of the codex is a perfect example of the acceptance of an information storage medium which is fit for purpose. Easy to make, easy to store and easy to use, the codex had every possible advantage over the scroll. Its cultural, religious and ultimately political overtones simply served to make it even more acceptable. Like the alphabet, once Europe had adopted the codex it never abandoned it, and it was to become one of the symbols of European influence in the non-European world from the 15th century onwards.

The codex has proved to have a longer active life than the materials from which the first codices were made. Vellum and parchment were both ultimately replaced by paper, while papyrus could never be used for codices at all because of its fragility when folded. Paper, unlike papyrus, is a product which undergoes a long and complicated manufacturing process during which the vegetable fibres from which it is made are physically and chemically modified. They are reduced to a pulp with water, and then reconstituted by drying in flat sheets. When the surface is sized, the material can take ink, and the sheet can be unfolded or rolled, and, provided that the materials are reasonably free of chemical impurities and the conditions of storage are reasonably good, it can be stored for long periods of time.

Paper was invented in China at the beginning of the fifth century CE, and the use of it, and the knowledge of the craft of paper-making, spread gradually westwards during the next thousand years. At first it came along the ancient trade routes that linked east and west across the steppes and mountains of what are now the states of central Asia. It reached western Asia at the time of the great Arab cultural expansion in the first century of Islam, and was taken by the Arabs throughout their burgeoning Empire in North Africa and southern Europe. From Spain and Italy it made its way northwards, until, by the 15th century, paper-making and the use of paper were well established throughout southern and western Europe. On the whole, however, it was used for less formal purposes; for formal or important documents, vellum and parchment were still common.

The alphabet, the codex and paper proved to be a formidable combination as an information storage and retrieval system. This was even more true when they were combined with a new system of 'writing' the alphabet on the paper. Writing was a manual process, whether the implement was a stylus, a chisel, a brush or a pen. In China, in the 11th century CE, a form of printing had been invented which involved making reproductions from engraved wooden blocks, a format particularly suited to the vast number of pictographs and syllabaries which, by that time, formed the Chinese character set. The process was adopted in Korea (which used a similar character set), but spread no further, and seems to have remained unknown in the West.

Printing: the first communications revolution

Printing in Europe was invented independently, in the 15th century. The earliest experiments may indeed have been with wooden blocks, but the breakthrough was the realization that the languages written in the Latin alphabet could be printed using only a very small number of characters. The inventor of typographic printing was Johann Gutenberg, a German goldsmith who, with various financial backers, printed the first European book, an edition of the Bible in Latin (1454-5). Gutenberg invented devices for making type as multiple copies of individual raised letters on the upper surface of small pieces of lead, and also various techniques for combining these, applying ink to them and imprinting their image on a suitable surface. The most suitable surface soon proved to be paper. The invention of printing sounded the death knell of parchment and vellum as the normal material for books and documents in Europe.

The rapid spread of the art of printing marked the beginning of a period of profound, even revolutionary, cultural change in the West. Printed books could be produced in great quantities, and were therefore both more widely available and cheaper than their hand-made predecessors. Moreover, every copy of the same edition was identical with every other copy, which allowed a whole series of aids to the use of books to be developed: the index, the citation, the bibliographical record. Because paper was so easy to use for books, and so comparatively strong and adaptable, formats became smaller, books became lighter and more portable and hence even cheaper and even more convenient. The codex itself survived as the normal form of the western book.

The written word, in printed form, became an integral part of life for the first time, a fact whose importance cannot be overemphasized. Print was an apparently far more stable medium than manuscript, and certainly more uniform. It was used by rulers and rebels alike in every sphere of life. No subject of the king could claim to be ignorant of the law when laws were accurately and identically disseminated in printed form. A religious or political dissident could reach a far larger audience when ideas could be circulated in print than had ever been possible when the range was limited either by personal contact and speech or by the production of handwritten copies. Scholars could read the work of other scholars whom they would never meet, and could study the very sources which had been used when an identical printed version lay upon the desks in front of them. Print transformed many aspects of the cultural, religious and political life of Europe.

The tradition of learning which western Europe had inherited from the ancient world was essentially repetitive rather than critical. Partly under the influence of the Church, which was paramount in all intellectual life for more than a thousand years, enquiry and experimentation were discouraged. Each generation learned what a previous generation had learned before, and little was added to the store of human knowledge and understanding. Originality was discouraged, and if it was achieved its dissemination could easily be prevented. Printing changed that forever. It became possible to compare, to contrast and to analyse on a far greater scale. Variant texts of sacred and secular works alike could be edited and reconciled into a standard, accepted version, which anyone could read and criticize. Scholars who, before the invention of printing, might never have seen more than a few score books in their lives, could now consult libraries containing thousands of books, printed throughout Europe, and written by those who, like themselves, had ever easier access to the growing store of knowledge. Printing provoked the first information explosion.

To contain, exploit and control the potential of print, new mechanisms and new institutions had to be devised. Containment was barely possible. Both secular and ecclesiastical authorities throughout Europe tried to clamp down on printing, but it spread inexorably across the continent. If it could not be suppressed, it could, however, be controlled; censorship by Church and State was an integral part of the world of the printed word almost from its very beginning. Exploitation could take many forms. Those who were censors could use the new medium to propagate their own views, and they did so shamelessly, both in Church and State. Indeed, the very idea of the centralized, bureaucratized nation-state developed in parallel with the spread of printing. But there was another form of exploitation, perhaps more positive, which gave more people access to books and information. After the great religious divide between Protestant and Catholic in the middle of the 16th century, one group - the Protestants - emphasized the need for literacy. In turn, this led to the creation of new and more inclusive systems of education, and the foundation of libraries, great and small, through which a new educated elite could be created. The process proved unstoppable once it had started, and as print became more integrated into the life of the West, literacy ceased to be a luxury and became a necessity. The invention of printing was a factor in all of this and more, demonstrating, perhaps for the first time, the power which accrues to those who control and have access to information and the concomitant disadvantage of those who do not. Knowledge became cumulative, as each generation added to the store, and recorded its findings and its opinions in a permanent and easily retrievable form, which at last began to realize the full potential of the alphabet as a means of storing linguistic information.

Printing technology was designed for reproducing alphabetic systems, and is less suitable for other forms of representation. The pictographic and syllabaric scripts of Asia have always presented a problem to printers, a fact which had important consequences as Europe began to impose its cultural domination on much of the rest of the world. Musical notation and even mathematical symbols similarly presented difficulties (although by no means insuperable ones) to printers, and the reproduction of graphic matter remained a problem for 300 years after the death of Gutenberg. In other words, despite its obvious advantages, printing was a limited medium, but because of its ubiquity, it turned western Europe into a culture dominated by what it could do so easily: reproduce written language. Oral culture, although never entirely lost, was submerged, and both the visual and the aural became parallel and separate experiences from the linguistic. Hence literacy, which had to be acquired by learning, became the basic skill of the western elite, while the more natural skills of seeing and hearing were, to some extent, devalued as mechanisms for information transfer.

For 400 years, printing was the dominant information transfer medium, and for much of that time it was unchallenged. Perhaps for that very reason, further development of the technology was slow. Mechanical power (first steam and then electricity) was applied to the printing press itself in the 19th century, and machine processes replaced handcrafts in paper-making at the same time, but it was not until the 20th century that mechanical systems entirely displaced typesetting by hand, and there are, to this day, some hand processes in the binding of books. The intense conservatism of the book-making industry – paper-making, printing and binding – reflects the unassailable position which the industry has occupied in the storage and dissemination of information for almost the whole of its history.

The trade in books

The dominance of print also had economic consequences. The gradual evolution of both religious and secular writing in the cultures bordering on the Mediterranean, and further east in both India and China, had, over many centuries, increased the knowledge of reading and writing, and gradually brought it closer to the commercial arena. In Greece, books were undoubtedly bought and sold; in Rome, by the first century BCE, there was a flourishing trade in them. They were copied by professional scriveners, sold by booksellers, and even commissioned by 'publishers'. The book trade, such as it was, vanished with the Roman Empire in the West, but it survived in Byzantium, and independently re-emerged in Paris in the 12th century. In due course, in many western cities, profes-sional scribes copied manuscripts for students and scholars, and soon for a few secular customers as well, so that by the middle of the 15th century there was an established book trade in almost all the larger towns of western Europe.

It may well be that it was the demand for books generated by this trade that motivated Gutenberg and others to experiment with a mechanical means which would replace the slow and tedious process of writing by hand every book which was required by a customer. Whether or not this was the case (and it seems likely that it was), the fact remains that the printed book was born into a world in which books were already indissolubly linked with commerce. The process of printing itself ensured that the link could never be broken. Even at the simplest level, a printer needed type, ink, a press and paper, as well as the necessary skills to make use of them. From the beginning, the printing trade needed capital investment, which could only be recouped over the medium term by the sale of the product. This taught harsh lessons to some printers: Gutenberg was not only the first typographic printer, he was also the first printer to go bankrupt.

Books produced in such unprecedentedly large numbers could not find a large enough market where they were produced, as the products of commercial scriptoria normally had. A bookselling network developed throughout western and southern Europe, based on existing trading routes and trade fairs. By the middle of the 16th century, there was a system of book distribution which allowed books to travel from one end of the continent to the other with little commercial impediment. This served to emphasize the book as an object of commerce, and the information that it contained, therefore, as having some monetary value. The book trade, as it spread across and beyond Europe, and vastly increased in size, became a massive contributor to the economic as well as the cultural life of the 19th and 20th centuries.

The enmeshment of the printed word in the development of capitalist economies inevitably put another obstacle between many people and information which they wanted or needed. By the 19th century, and in some cases earlier, social and political reformers recognized that they could only reach the masses through the printed word if the forms of print were cheap enough for them to buy and common enough to justify the time and effort of learning to read and sustaining their literacy. Education, book provision and political change became closely associated in the minds of many radicals from the 17th century onwards, but never more so than during the 19th century when the partial mechanization of the printing industry brought the price of books and newspapers down to realistic levels for less wealthy buyers and readers. At the same time, governments used fiscal devices as a form of censorship, taxing newspapers and other reading matter in an attempt to prevent the wide circulation of radical ideas. Although this policy was gradually abandoned from the middle of the century onwards in many countries in western Europe, both taxation and formal censorship survived in many other parts of the world.

The 19th century saw the high point of the dominance of western culture by print. A combination of economic, technical, social and political circumstances made the printed word seem to be the unique instrument of cultural enrichment and even cultural change. No other medium could challenge its capacity to record and reproduce information, while the printed book was a uniquely efficient instrument of information retrieval. Great libraries of such books were the storehouses of the world's knowledge, whether in private hands or accessible to a wider public. Yet as print achieved these pinnacles, the process of displacement began.

Even at the height of its domination, print never displaced the spoken word as the most common means of human communication and information transfer. Orality has always been a parallel skill to literacy, and for most people, throughout most of history, far more important. Much of the knowledge that we need in our daily lives has been acquired orally and by example, from the simplest skills which we were taught as children to the immense complexity of the use of language itself. Even as a formal mechanism for the transmission of information, orality was never entirely displaced. The lecture survived (perhaps for too long) the invention of the textbook. The spoken word was integral to the development of democratic processes, looking back to the partially pre-literate societies of Greece and Rome. In a society in which illiteracy was common (as it was in much of the West until the last quarter of the 19th century) orality remained an essential tool of social intercourse and social control, but if language was to be preserved it had to be written down and perhaps printed.

Chapter 2

Mass media and new technology

The pictorial image

During the second half of the 19th century, there began a new stage in the evolution of the storage and communication of information. It can be seen as an attempt to overcome some of the inflexibility of print, tied as it was to the alphabetic representation of language and a few other sets of symbols such as those used by musicians or mathematicians. The earliest experiments were with processes that facilitated the reproduction of visual images in print. Such processes had existed since the 15th century, and indeed the simplest of them – the carved wooden block – had probably been invented in Europe before typographic printing and had certainly been in use in east Asia for centuries before the first book was printed in the West. Woodcuts were crude but could be effective; indeed the woodcuts that allegedly illustrated the martyrdom of English Protestants in the reign of Mary I (1553–1558) became one of the most common visual images of the past for millions of people in the following 200 years.

At a more sophisticated and technically satisfying level, a printing process that made it possible to reproduce engravings made on metal (usually copper) plates was developed in the 16th century. This process was in use, with some modifications and refinements, for 200 years; engravers reached a high level of technical and artistic achievement. At the very end of the 18th century, another new printing process, lithography, made it possible for the artist to draw an image on a prepared block of stone (or later of metal) which could then be reproduced without any further intervention from an engraver or woodcutter. However, all of these processes, even woodcut, were expensive, and, except in the very best of hands, reproductions were little more than approximations to the subjects they allegedly portrayed.

From the 1840s onwards, the invention of photography changed this forever. Although the early processes were expensive, cumbersome and unreliable, within 30 years a means had been found of reproducing photographs in print. By the end of the 19th century they were beginning to appear in some of the more popular newspapers. Long before then, photographs of famous places and people had become a part of daily life, quite apart from the use of photography for more personal purposes as an expensive, but increasingly popular, hobby. Photography created a new view of the world. A photograph was assumed to be accurate, and it allowed people to 'see' things that they would never see in reality, without any mediation or interpretation by an artist or an engraver. This directness, however, was more apparent than real. Photography, like most of the media that followed it, required operators with technical skills not only in the creation of the image itself but also in processing it to make it visible to the viewer. That process could itself 'improve' or modify the image. Photography did nevertheless open up another aspect of the world, just as printing had done 400 years earlier, for, like printing, it overcame some of the barriers of time and distance in the transmission of information. It also had its own inherent technical and economic obstacles to the full exploitation of its potential. Photography began the revolution in visual information.

The recording and transmission of sound

The invention of recording and the development of telegraphy and wireless gave a new importance to orality. At first, sound recording was little more than a toy for the rich, used almost entirely for the recording of music. The problem of transmitting sound over distance needed to be resolved in a different way. The first electro-mechanical device to achieve this was the electric telegraph developed in the early 19th century and brought into use in 1844. Its coded messages, important as they were in government, business and news gathering, could never have the same immediacy of impact as voice transmission, but telegraph cables were laid all over

Europe and North America, and ultimately between continents, to provide the first system of instantaneous communication over distances beyond the limits of human vision. The telephone (invented in 1876) was a great advance on the telegraph, by allowing direct spoken communication. By the end of the 19th century, it was becoming common in North America, and beginning to be used in Europe.

The telephone, like photography, was for the rich, although it was always more than a social toy. The obvious use of both telegraphy and telephony in business and in government made them a matter of public concern as photography had never been. The obvious potential of both systems made them as interesting to late 19th-century governments as printing had been to the authorities of early 16th-century Europe. Just as the bishops and princes of the Renaissance had reacted to printing by censoring the printed word, the governments of the later 19th century reacted to the invention of the telegraph and telephone by developing state-owned or state-controlled networks of cables and exchanges and even equipment. It became common practice to associate telegraphy and telephony with postal services; the combination of Post, Telegraph and Telephone, known as PTT, remains the norm in many parts of the world. In most countries state intervention did not lead to censorship, although in a few it did, and everywhere it opened up the possibility of monitoring telephone conversations. Only in the USA was a purely commercial telephone system permitted, but even there the companies were partially regulated under federal and state laws. Around the world, two forms of regulation were developed: the American model, which involved the state only as regulator, and the other, common in Europe, which involved state ownership of the infrastructure of telecommunications. In Britain, telephones were a virtual monopoly of the state PTT provider, the Post Office, almost from their first introduction until 1982; this pattern was replicated in many countries.

Mass media: radio and cinema

Wireless broadcasting was the second great contributor to the development of the oral communications culture of the 20th century. Another invention of the late 19th century, it had two basic uses. It could be used for communications from one person to another, rather like a telephone but with a different technology, or it could be used for communication from one person to many people, provided that all of the would-be recipients of the signal had appropriate equipment on which to receive it. It was the latter principle – broadcasting – that was to become of paramount importance. Wireless broadcasting of both speech and music was established in western Europe and North America by the mid-1920s (and earlier in some countries) and rapidly became an integral part of daily life. Here there was indeed a formidable challenge to the primacy of print on many fronts. The broadcasters could at the same time beat the printed newspapers in the immediacy of their coverage and occupy the leisure time that might otherwise have been devoted to reading books. Broadcasting could be used for education, as well as for entertainment and information. It gave politicians and others a new means of reaching those whom they wished to influence. In some countries, broadcasting became a prime medium for advertising, and in others for political and religious propaganda. Some governments took charge of this powerful new medium and carefully controlled access to it. Some developed regulatory regimes which tried to protect the independence of the broadcasters and a few allowed it into an almost entirely commercial sphere. Everywhere, however, the potency and influence of the new medium was recognized and acknowledged.

The commercial success of sound broadcasting meant that it was possible to manufacture receivers at a price that large numbers of people could afford. The wireless (it did not become the 'radio' in popular speech in Britain until the 1960s) took its place in almost every western home during the 1930s. It became a vital instrument of information and opinion-forming before and during World War II.

The other great popular medium of that period, although one which was perhaps used more for entertainment than for information, was the cinema. Moving pictures had first been made in the 1890s, and a small industry had begun to develop around their production and distribution before World War I. By 1920, the centre of that industry was the USA, although a number of European countries, including Britain, continued to be serious players in the market. From the mid-1920s onwards, however, American money, talent and ideas dominated the cinema throughout the world except where governments tried to prevent or limit the import or exhibition of American films. The addition of sound to the formerly silent images (which were in fact always accompanied by live music in the cinema) in 1927 completed the creation of a new and powerful information medium. Film was to be one of the most potent mechanisms for propaganda in the 1930s and World War II in both the democracies and the dictatorships.

These new media were beginning to undermine both the unique position of print and the cultural self-confidence of its advocates by the end of the 1930s. The pleasure to be obtained from listening to the radio or watching a film was, for many people, as great as or greater than that from reading a book, and perhaps demanded less effort and fewer skills. Information acquired through a broadcast or a film was similarly 'easy'; it soon came to be regarded as being as authoritative as the printed word. The new media, however, were monolithic in a way in which the printed word had never been, at least in comparatively open societies. Even in the democracies, the economics of both broadcasting and film-making effectively dictated the creation of monopolies or near-monopolies. The British compromise of a politically independent public sector monopoly broadcaster was a model that found no significant imitators. Even in Britain, it could not be applied to the cinema with its dependence on American suppliers of films. The infrastructure of both broadcasting and cinema was so expensive that only the very rich, or large well capitalized companies, could truly compete in the mass market. In both production and distribution in the film industry, it was the large-scale capitalists who succeeded, and thus were born the media giants which characterize so much of the global communications and information industry at the beginning of the 21st century.

Television

Influential as they were, sound broadcasting and the cinema had their limitations. The former made its impact by being instantaneous (and sometimes even spontaneous, though rarely so in Britain) and in the home;

the latter did so by its use of powerful visual images, emotive music and evocation of a lifestyle far beyond the reach of the vast majority of its audience. Television, the last and greatest of the 20th-century mass media, did both. It was at once domestic and universal, instantaneous and ubiquitous. From very tentative beginnings in 1936, television became, within little more than 30 years, the most universal and most powerful medium of communication and information yet invented. Like radio, it could be used and misused by governments and commercial interests alike. It could also, however, convey images of potent immediacy, whether of an assassination or a football match. It irreversibly changed the way in which people lived throughout the world, and how they perceived that world.

Like radio and the cinema, television broadcasting needs a complex and costly infrastructure, although in real terms the cost began to fall in the 1980s as new miniaturized digital technologies became widely available. In practice, however, there has been limited opportunity for competition in the television industry. Even countries which have a fundamentally free market, such as the USA, also have a regulatory regime and some control over output. At the very least, such a regulatory regime has an oversight of content to prevent the broadcasting of material which is harmful or offensive. Of course, these terms are subjective, and the extent of content control of television output varies greatly between countries and over periods of time. It is not, however, normal for democracies to have monopoly service providers in the television industry whether of content or networks. In most western countries, state broadcasters compete with the private sector, sometimes funded by advertising for which they also have to compete. Only in the late 1980s, with the global spread of satellite and cable systems, did a serious element of less controlled competition enter into the television industry. For most of its history so far, television has emphasized and probably hastened the development of monopolistic commercial control of the communication of information.

Taken together, the mass media of the 20th century enriched and enhanced the lives of hundreds of millions of people throughout the world. Despite the foreboding of moralists, the fears of governments and the complaints of a partially displaced cultural elite (all of them with some justification), cinema, radio and, above all, television gave more access to more information to more people than at any time in history. Moreover, the traditional information industry of the printed word has survived the assault. It has changed, perhaps fundamentally (a theme that will be further explored in Chapter 3), but all the various media, including print, have a role in the global information and communication economy. As we begin to be able to develop an historical perspective, we can perhaps see that the mass media of the 20th century have supplemented rather than displaced the printed word. They do best the things which it does badly or not at all: they have visual and aural impact, they have immediacy, they have ease of access, they have universality. Together, the mass media have revived and extended the oral and visual culture which was almost lost in the world of print. Even those who are regular readers now absorb much of their knowledge of current affairs from radio and television, and newspapers have adapted themselves accordingly. Musical performances, sporting events, even the proceedings of parliaments, which were once directly available only to the few and could reach the majority only in a reported form, are now directly visible and audible to almost everyone. If it can be argued that print facilitated the process of democratization in Europe, it can be as cogently suggested that the mass media have the potential to complete that process throughout the world.

Computers: the second communications revolution

The mass media offer a supplement to print, but have displaced only its less effective applications. The same may not be quite so true of the effects of the most recent revolutionary change in the information world, that based on the use of computers.

Attempts to make mechanical devices to assist in mathematical calculations are almost as old as mathematics itself. The abacus was widely used in China a thousand years ago, and is still in use there today. Most famously, in the 1830s, Charles Babbage designed, but never built, what he called a 'difference engine' in which the movements of mechanical parts were determined by logical sequences which followed from the operation of particular keys. We know that Babbage's engine would have worked; one was built at the Science Museum, London, in 1991. The design incorporated the essential principle of building a machine which would respond in a predetermined (or 'programmed') way to a particular set of circumstances. The concept has to be linked to a power source to drive the machine; this was not achieved until the middle of the 20th century, although mathematicians and others continued to work on the problem of how to solve problems which were too complicated or simply too big for conventional calculation.

The impetus for the creation of an electro-mechanical device to do this came from the impact of war in the 1940s. The need to break the codes used by the Germans for their military wireless traffic forced British scientists to develop machines that could take random sequences of letters and find the logical sequences which had to exist if the signal had any meaning. The machines that were ultimately developed to do this were also capable of being programmed to undertake mathematical calculations and other logical operations. The writing and application of logical programs was, and remains, the basis of computing. There have, however, been two great changes. The first is the storage capacity of the computers themselves – their ability to 'remember' information – and their capacity to process the information which is held in the memory. The second is the development of a linkage between computing and telecommunications systems, which enables computers to 'talk' to each other and thus to access each other's memory banks and processing power. It was the latter, usually called information technology, which underpinned the information and communication revolution of the last two decades of the 20th century that is being carried forward into the new millennium.

Although computers emerged out of a combination of scientific curiosity and the imperatives of war, their evolution after World War II began to give them the potential to operate outside the military and scientific spheres. Indeed, there was a suite of problems for which they were to prove an ideal solution. Since the late 19th century, developments in two hitherto unrelated fields had created issues that could only be solved by the more effective management of information. The first was in the commercial world. Both in manufacturing and in sales, business was becoming more complicated. Science-based industrial processes that were only economic to run on a very large scale – as in the chemical industry, for example – meant that companies had become larger, had more employees and were employing many different kinds of specialists. In the commercial sector in general, the need for better record keeping for everything from stock inventory to employee entitlements (which were themselves beginning to take on a modern level of complexity) forced companies to consider how such records were to be created, stored and retrieved. The adoption of the typewriter and the telephone were the harbingers of change, but the development of semi-automatic information systems (punched cards, for example, or even the humble card index) pointed the way towards more complex later developments.

The second group of issues emerged in the world of science. Science was becoming more complex, more specialized and more international. Its literature was already undergoing exponential growth, as specialist journals proliferated and specialisms themselves became narrower and more intensive. Science was more than an academic pursuit; long before World War II, when its military applications were urgent and overt, it was seen as a vital element in national defence strategies as well as in wealth creation. Effective intellectual and physical access to scientific literature became an economic and political necessity in which the state began to play a part through its support not only of research but also of libraries which supported research.

Gradually a solution to the two apparently divergent sets of problems emerged, which was, in effect, the development of what was later to be called information management. Large companies began to employ people whose job it was to manage information by creating systems which enabled it to be systematically stored and efficiently retrieved. By the late 1930s there was a recognizable profession developing around these activities within major enterprises in many sectors, both public and private. The capacity of computers to handle information was a matter of urgent interest to those information managers who could see their potential in the years immediately following World War II. The coming together of the new technology and a whole range of scientific and commercial problems was the driving force of the computer-led revolution which transformed social, economic and political life in the following half century.

The first problem that needed to be addressed was to find an effective means by which people and computers could communicate with each other. Almost from the beginning this was through a keyboard based on the familiar design of the typewriter. In the earliest computers, the keystrokes made holes of predetermined patterns in strips of paper or in cards. Each letter or number was represented by a unique combination of holes. A mechanical device then 'read' this into the computer, where each combinzation of holes was converted into an equivalent expressed in terms of a binary number, which allowed the computer to perform its logical operations by a series of decisions between two alternatives, 'yes' and 'no'. It was a clumsy system, both time-consuming and inaccurate, in which hours of keyboarding were followed by hours of proofreading and yet more hours of tedious corrections.

For 20 years after their invention, computers largely remained the tools of science, and principally of expensive 'big' science. They were used for vastly complex calculations in mathematics and physics, and for little else. Commercial uses were only slowly explored, the pioneers being big companies whose business involved handling large quantities of numerical data; in practice, this meant banks, insurance companies and a few other very large corporations. Gradually, however, computing came to be used for data which were not primarily numeric. The reason for the adoption of the computer in business, industry and government, as well as in its academic applications, lay in its ability to make perfect matches between identical data, while rejecting all attempts to match non-identical data, and to retrieve a particular item of data with great speed from a store of almost unlimited size, as well as in its power to analyse and process data following the instructions in a program. Moreover, once data were stored in a form which the computer could read, the machine could, for example, identify all uses of a particular word, and be programmed to show that word (perhaps in some specified context) to the operator. This pointed the way towards the bibliographic application of computation to address the issues faced by scientific researchers and their information managers. Computers could retrieve words from bibliographies, or indeed from texts, and could print the context or the reference. In a different application, data on individuals could be stored, analysed and retrieved to reveal, for example, information about their spending habits or other aspects of their way of life, extending the potential of computers not merely into the academic social sciences but into key areas of information needed by government to develop policy and monitor its effectiveness.

Conceptually, all of this was understood by the pioneers of scientific computing in the late 1940s and early 1950s; some even envisaged a time when computers would be able to 'think' *illogically*, just like a human being. Both business and bibliographical applications developed during the 1960s, although only fitfully. The next phase of development, and the transformation of the computer into the ubiquitous tool of the 21st century, depended on the invention of two further devices, not available until the 1970s: the transistor and the semiconductor. Transistors were developed for use in radios in the 1950s, and were the basis of the portable radios that became common in the following decade. The properties of semicon-ductors, however, were investigated only in the 1960s, and it was not until ten years later that their potential was fully exploited. In essence, they facilitated the miniaturization of the memory of the computer, just as the transistor facilitated the miniaturization of its electronics. The 'microchip', made of silicon – the principal semiconductive material used in the computing industry – contained millions of miniaturized electrical circuits, each of which held the electronically memorized program for particular sets of operations. Some of these were basic and 'simple' (the order of the letters of the Latin alphabet, for example) while others were far more complex, involving mathematical functions, or the instructions necessary to run the computer itself, such as how to translate the operator's keystrokes into images on the screen.

The same developments finally dispensed with the paper tape and punch cards of the early days of computing. Input (still from a keyboard) was directly converted into digitized form and stored on an electromagnetic disk. The disks themselves were also miniaturized, until the standard format by the late 1980s had a diameter of only 3.5 inches, on which millions of digitized characters could be stored. Programs which ran particular operations on the computer were similarly stored, and could therefore supplement the basic memory of the machine itself, internally stored on the hard disk. As hard disks became more capacious the processing power of computers continued to increase exponentially. George Moore, Chairman of Intel, evolved 'Moore's Law', which stated that the pace of development of microchips meant that they in effect halved in size and doubled in capacity every 18 months; the practical effect is that the real-term costs of computers and computing has been falling continuously since the early 1980s. The computer thus became at once a more powerful and more flexible tool; data and programs alike could be taken from machine to machine, quite apart from the ability of machines to communicate directly with each other.

Microchips were the basis of the microcomputers that came onto the market in the late 1970s; they were sold at almost unimaginably low prices, and were easy to use even for those with no scientific expertise and no real understanding of computing itself. Within a decade, the computer had become as familiar as print had been to earlier generations. Computers became smaller as they became cheaper and more powerful. The minicomputer of the 1970s, taking up a small room and presided over by priest-like specialists wearing white coats and speaking an arcane language, was displaced by a desktop machine no larger than a television, and, in due course, by a genuinely portable laptop computer. Hand-held easily portable devices followed in the early years of the 21st century. The image and the reality of computers were soon to be found everywhere. Machines which dispensed money appeared in the walls of banks. Clocks and watches changed in the way in which they showed the time. Working practices changed in almost every shop, office and factory in the industrialized world. Libraries were transformed. Instant information had arrived.

Much of this information was no longer held in the memory of the computer that was used to retrieve it or on a disk inserted into it. Networks began to be developed for military and commercial purposes in the 1960s, and gradually became more common. The essence of a network is that digitized signals are sent from one computer, by cables or microwaves similar to those used for telephones, in a format that can be understood by another computer at the other end of the line. In this way, the user of the recipient computer can gain access to both the information and the processing power of the transmitting, or host, computer, although in practice this is often restricted by the providers of the data and the services. Networks are the infrastructural foundation of the information society. Some, especially in the academic world, are almost common-user systems like the telephone network. Others are more restricted and may be expensive to use: some are commercially provided; some are private, restricted to employees of a particular company or government department; some, no doubt, are wholly secret. The great 'network of networks', the internet, has become a familiar feature of contemporary life and perhaps our most important single system of communication.

Networks are designed primarily to provide access to information in 'real time', that is, the request for information and the response to it are immediately consecutive. The information itself is stored in a database, which is structured so that selected data can be retrieved from it. As with a book, the intellectual quality of the structure will determine the ease and effectiveness of the retrieval process. Because of the speed at which computers work and their ability to match like with like, searching for and retrieving information has always been one of their primary functions. In the early days of computer use in information work, the search was typically for a single term (rather like using a book index), or for a combination of terms. The latter, using a system of logic called 'Boolean algebra', was established by the mid-1970s as the normal search technique. A Boolean search allows the user to combine terms, but also to exclude other terms from the parameters of the search, using the concepts of AND, OR and NOT. These 'Boolean operators' therefore permit the construction of such requests as 'literature AND English', which will generate references to 'English literature'. How effectively a Boolean search can be conducted depends, however, on how well the database itself is constructed; in some cases, the database is so complex that the user needs to have attained an almost professional standard of skill in searching in order to make effective use of it.

The development of information retrieval as a new skill of librarians and other information workers was an important development of the 1970s and early 1980s, but the systems continued to present serious difficulties to non-expert users. The search was on for some means of circumventing the complexities of Boolean methods, and, at the same time, of using ordinary language rather than complicated predetermined vocabularies of acceptable terms. A solution was found in the development of the system known as hypertext, conceptualized by Ted Nelson in the 1960s but not fully realized until the 1980s. The essence of hypertext is that it permits the user to make a series of consecutive searches without having to define a precise search term. This is achieved by building links into the database which allow the user to go from one place to the next without any intervening steps. Thus, the user seeking information on Shakespeare may find a reference in the retrieved text to 'Globe Theatre'; if the user understands this reference, no action is taken, but if the reference is unknown, or more information is sought, a simple click on the mouse will automatically call up the relevant part of the database, from which the user can then return, at will, to the main text. This facility – electronic browsing – is fundamental to hypertext technology and, as we shall see in Chapter 4, to the development of the world wide web.

The application of the hypertext principle is not, however, confined to textual databases. Since the mid-1980s, databases have become multi-media objects. The essence of multimedia is that it contains not merely text, but also images (still or moving) and sound (speech, music, natural sounds, and so on). All of this is digitized, and can therefore – with appropriate indexing – be searched, or can be found through hypertext links. Hypermedia – the multimedia version of hypertext – is the basis of many contemporary databases, and has made the combination of words, images and sounds familiar to the users of information. Although the earlier audiovisual media combined the aural and the visual, they lacked the crucial element of searchability which makes digitized multimedia databases such powerful reference tools. Encyclopedias, atlases and similar works of reference, as well as highly specialized training tools in fields as diverse as engineering and surgery, are increasingly published in multimedia rather than printed or audio visual formats.

The normal format for portable multimedia objects became the optical disc, familiar as the compact disc or CD. The CD first came into general use as a medium for recorded sound of extraordinarily high quality, and has almost entirely displaced the earlier recorded sound formats such as magnetic tape and vinyl discs. An optical disc, however, can be used for any digitized data. The data on the audio CD is retrieved by a sound system, which translates it into audio signals played through amplifiers and loud-speakers. In exactly the same way, the digitized data in a textual database can be retrieved through a computer system and displayed on a screen. This was developed commercially as the CD-ROM (compact disc – read only memory), which by the mid-1990s was familiar in almost all libraries and a growing number of businesses and homes. The CD-ROM need not be solely textual. Multimedia CD-ROMs became common, for it was they that provided the format for such electronic works of reference as dictionaries, encyclopedias and other familiar tools that were converted into electronic form in the 1990s. The combination of CD-ROM and hypermedia is a powerful one; indeed, it was the most powerful information retrieval tool that had ever been made available to all but a handful of professional users.

At the turn of the 21st century the digital variable disc (DVD) brought digitization to home entertainment. Commercial DVDs are more than digitized versions of movies. They typically include background inform-ation, commentary and perhaps critical analyses of the film that is the core content of the disc. The DVD is now displacing the video (itself barely 20 years old as a domestic device) as the medium for repeated access to movies. Recordable DVDs and writable CDs will further enhance their impact. The flash drive, or data stick, came into widespread use from about 2005 onwards. Taking advantage of the standardized USB port on all desktop and laptop computers, it has become the normal mode of physical transport for data, and, together with writable CDs, has given individuals further control over their own content. The pace of technological innovation, and the apparently insatiable desire to use new media, show no sign of diminishing.

The effects of the digital revolution are being felt far beyond the narrow confines of the world of information storage and retrieval. The DVD is merely one example of the transformative consequences of the technology. Conventional communications systems have also been changed almost beyond recognition. The telephone, the Victorian device which created the telecommunications industry, has been one of the greatest beneficiaries. A wide range of services is now offered by telecommunications companies themselves, often in competition with one another, quite apart from the

almost limitless services that can be obtained over the telephone from banking through mail order shopping to entertainment services of varying
degrees of social acceptability. Digital exchanges have replaced the old
electromechanical devices, and direct dialling across the world is commonplace. We can make calls using credit cards and charge cards, store and
retrieve numbers and make use of a dozen other systems that were unknown
little more than a decade ago. The touch-tone telephone makes all this
possible by digitizing the tones and transmitting them as messages to
computers.

Perhaps the greatest revolution in personal telecommunications has
been the mobile, or cellular, phone. This too is a child of the digital
revolution both in its hardware and in the networks. If the mobile phone
is not always regarded as an unmixed blessing, it is nevertheless the case
that it has become essential to the private and professional lives of
hundreds of millions of people across the globe. The internet can be
accessed from a mobile phone, and the portable battery-operated computer
used together with the mobile phone has the potential to free us from the
office, the classroom, or any other fixed location for working, learning and
communicating. The impact of this next phase of the digital revolution on
our habits of education, work and leisure can already be imagined, and is
already being partly realized. Mobile technology is personalized technology;
through a single device we can access most of the information and
communication systems that we need for any purpose, at a time of our own
choice and in a place and format that we want.

Meanwhile, the mass media are also being changed by digitization.
Digital radio and television have brought a higher technical quality of
reception than has been possible before, and at the same time opened up
the possibility of hundreds of new channels limited only by the
availability of frequencies and bandwidth. Again, this may not be seen as
an unmixed blessing, but as the technologies become more common and
the cost of acquiring and using them falls, the prospect of truly
community-based broadcasting becomes more real. This can lead to
radically wider access to television, still the most powerful of the mass
media. The music industry is also subject to the pressure of change.
Having pioneered the commercial use of optical discs in the move from

vinyl records to CD, the industry now finds itself the victim of the availability of digital sound through the internet. Both legally and illegally, this is becoming probably the most common means to access recently issued popular music, to the extent that performers and producers are moving away from the use of CD towards online distribution, to the economic detriment of the music retailers. The whole industry is facing the need to reassess and rebuild its business models.

An image of instantaneous worldwide access to information would, however, be somewhat deceptive. Behind the new information revolution lies an industry that is capital-intensive and highly competitive. Instant information is indeed available if the owners of the information would make it so, and if the seekers were able to gain access to it. The vast costs of installing computer systems are inevitably passed on to the customers of millions of businesses. There is human cost in the retraining of staff (not always successfully) to use the new technology. Some formerly high-level tasks – even some professional occupations – have been de-skilled. A global industry looks globally for its workforce; jobs have been exported from the West to Asia and to eastern Europe. The new industry, either directly or indirectly, has absorbed much of the surplus capital in western countries. Moreover, some of the promises have failed. Even now, not all computers, and certainly not all software, are reliable, idiot-proof and user-friendly, even when allegedly designed for non-expert users. Instant information is indeed available to the money dealer or the stockbroker – at a very high price – but information systems for the domestic market have so far been only a limited success. Some of the democratizing effects of the revolutions in communications and information are even apparently in danger of being reversed. Access to information is increasingly dependent on wealth and skills to an extent that has not been true in the world of print since the 19th century, nor in the mass media for most of their existence. The gap between rich and poor, at both personal and national levels, has become more marked. In countries where the PTT networks were not well developed, network-based technologies re-emphasize the divide and the barriers, although the development of cellular networks even in comparatively poor countries (where they are cheaper to install and maintain than conventional hard-wired systems) is beginning to address this issue.

That is the paradox. Technology has made more information more available to more people than at any time in tens of thousands of years of human history. But the same technology has made access to it more difficult. It is that paradox, and some of its implications, which subsequent chapters seek to explore.

PART 2
The economic dimension

Chapter 3

The information market-place

The publishing industry: a paradigm of information transfer

The mechanisms that have been developed for the transfer of information from source to user all require significant capital investment. The role of information in society can only be properly understood in a context in which its cost and monetary value are properly taken into account. The development of information technology, and the gradual convergence of previously separate technologies, have tended to emphasize both the cost of the infrastructure of information systems and that of delivering the service to the user. But this is not entirely new. The change, although it is significant and even radical, has been one of degree rather than of kind. As we saw in Chapter 1, ever since the invention of printing, and in a very limited way even before that, there has been an overtly commercial element in the information transfer process. The trade in the printed word is perhaps not the only comparison which could be used as a model for the commercialization of computer-based information service provision, but it is certainly the most familiar. Print, in all its manifestations, is still the most common, and arguably remains the most important, information medium in terms of the quantity of stored information which is uniquely available and the comparative ease of access which it offers. It is, therefore, with print that we shall begin.

The publishing industry – the producer of books, magazines and newspapers – is merely one part of a larger complex of trades and industries. The size and scale of the operation of individual firms within this complex varies from vast multinational corporations, such as News Corporation, at one extreme, to a small bookshop owned and operated by a single person at the other. Linking these improbable partners is a long chain of supply which provides the route along which information can travel from source to user. Inevitably, however, the chain is continuously subjected to commercial pressures, and the free flow of information itself may sometimes be distorted or disrupted by accident or design. In other words, the financial parameters within which publishing (like all the other sectors of the information industry) must work act as both an accelerator and a brake in the process of information supply.

The literal meaning of the verb 'to publish' is 'to make public', but in common usage it has taken on the more familiar sense of 'to issue copies of a book, magazine, newspaper, etc, for sale'. Although this is the only sensible way in which to use the word, it is important to remember its root meaning. At the heart of the publishing process lies the concept of *dissemination*. In the publishing industry, this means the dissemination of information which has been put into a material form. Historically this has been print on paper; but just as there was commercial book production before the invention of printing, there are now mechanisms of publishing which involve neither print nor paper. It is the process of translating information into a format and medium in which it can be put into public domain that defines the publishing industry.

Authors and publishers

A publisher is essentially an intermediary between author and reader. The process of knowledge creation and information dissemination begins, therefore, with the author. The 'author', however, is a concept as multifaceted as the 'publisher'. The classic model is of the individual using knowledge or imagination to create a text which in some way expresses what the author wishes to convey to the reader. It is a model derived essentially from the 'creative' writer, the poet or novelist, although it can certainly be applied to the authors of certain kinds of non-fiction as well. Few texts, however, are created wholly out of the imagination of the author. Many novelists undertake research; this may involve the study of subjects as diverse as social history or aircraft design depending on the subject matter of the book. Even where no formal research is undertaken, novelists are typically drawing on knowledge acquired by experience as well as relying on pure invention. The imaginative element often lies in the use made of knowledge, whether or not its acquisition is experiential.

As we move away from fiction, the authorial model gradually changes. In principle, a work of non-fiction might be written in a way which is not unlike writing a novel. An individual author researches a topic, analyses the material, reduces it to a logical and often narrative form, and composes the work. Indeed, this is the classic model of scholarship in the humanities and much of the writing of commercial non-fiction of the sort seen in bookshops and public libraries. Methods may vary between individual authors, partly because of their own habits and preferences, and partly because of the nature of their subjects and the sources of information which they use, but the variations are less important than the fundamental similarities.

In these two models, which represent the common understanding of how books are written, the commercial element may, at first sight, seem to be lacking. This is not the case, for the author must find someone who is willing to take the risk of turning the content of the created work into a form in which it can be distributed. Since authors are typically aiming at printed publication in the form of a book, that intermediary is the publisher, and it is to the publisher that the author sells the work. For some authors, the money received for that sale may be a minor consideration, but for many it is an important or even predominant factor. A popular novelist is essentially the producer of a highly profitable commodity. The commodity may have some cultural or literary value, if only as a socially acceptable form of entertainment, but it is nevertheless a commodity. The author may even enjoy the process of creating the commodity – the evidence is that most authors do – but that does not in itself change the fact that the activity is principally commercial. The same is true of almost all non-fiction; indeed, the vast majority of such books are commissioned by publishers from authors so that, at the time of writing, the author knows that the product, provided that it meets the publisher's expectations, will indeed be sold.

It might be argued that there is another model, in which the author of a work of literature or scholarship writes without thought of financial gain. There are indeed such authors, but even they are writing in the hope of being read because they believe they have something to say. Authors can, of course, try to circumvent the conventional channels of publication and distribution. So-called 'vanity' publishing – in which the author effectively pays for the publication of his work – is the most notorious manifestation of this, but there are more respectable methods. Publication by learned societies and university presses may attract *de facto* subsidies (sometimes as direct subventions, sometimes as subscriptions) to allow intrinsically worthwhile work to be published even though it is of limited commercial potential.

Since the late 1990s, the world wide web has come to be a widely used medium for the dissemination by authors of material which would not normally have found its way into print, or for which conventional printed publication is no longer economically viable. This – like so much of what happens on the internet – may sometimes be of questionable social, literary or scholarly value, but it does provide a genuinely different mechanism for an author to reach an audience. The use of the web in this way is opening up new possibilities for authors and publishers alike. Authors are no longer obliged to use commercial publication mechanisms to reach the limited readership which is normal for a literary novel or a scholarly monograph. It may continue to be professionally or culturally desirable to do so, but perceptions are changing, and online publication is beginning to be accorded equal status with print-on-paper. This, as we shall see, is particularly true in the academic and research communities, but specialist communities of all kinds are benefitting from online publishing. Moreover, the web is having a significant impact on print-on-paper publishing, as well as facilitating electronic publishing. The rapid development of e-commerce in the book trade since the late 1990s means that authors and publishers can reach individual book buyers without going through bookshops. This allows highly specialized titles to be marketed and sold directly to their small audience. Ironically, therefore, the adoption of web-based marketing and sales has made it easier for small publishers, and for individual authors, to advertise, market and sell their products.

We have, over some 500 years, created a chain of information supply in which the dissemination of the printed word can be achieved only by the exchange of money. In a networked environment, there are no free goods, but the source of the costs, and the responsibility for meeting them, are changing.

The commercial dimension is even more overt when we turn away from a 'simple' historical model of authorship. The author of a work of non-fiction may be helped by others who work as research assistants; the public acknowledgement of their roles can vary from a brief mention in a preface to a statement of joint authorship on the title-page. In the academic world a whole series of conventions and courtesies (which differ somewhat between disciplines) surround such matters; for other writers of non-fiction they are determined by personal inclination or contractual agreement. At one end of the scale is the paid researcher who provides the information from which the author fashions the book, and may be fully acknowledged as a joint or even coequal author; at the other is the ghost writer who actually writes the book but whose identity and existence may be wholly concealed from the reader. The concept of 'author' is far less easily defined when two or more people are the creators of a particular work, differing both in their inputs and in the public acknowledgement of their respective contributions.

As the group of contributors to authoring a work becomes larger, their relationships become more complex. The role of the publisher as financier of the operation then becomes even more important. Authors do not generally employ assistants or ghosts to work on books with them or for them unless publication is contractually guaranteed; in that case, the costs are effectively borne by the publisher. Where a work is avowedly of multiple authorship, the publisher's role is rather different. A volume of essays on a particular topic, for example, will typically be commissioned by a publisher from an editor. It is normally the editor's job to recruit a team of contributors; the editor then has an intellectual input to the creation of the work as a whole. The individual contributors, however, are directly contracted to the publisher by whom they are paid; the publisher's role is therefore principally commercial. In more complex cases, such as a major encyclopaedia, the editorial role may be undertaken by a team of people, perhaps with a body of advisers, and with a large number of contributors. The operation then has a major administrative dimension as well as an intellectual one.

These simple and familiar examples illustrate the variety and complexity of the publishing process even in its most basic relationship, that between the author and publisher of a printed book. If we turn to newspapers and consumer magazines (as opposed to scholarly journals), we find yet another set of relationships. Both of these forms of periodical have editors who normally have the authority to decide what will be printed and what will not. The authors, however, are journalists who, in many cases, are direct employees of the publishing house which owns the title. They are told what to write about, either generally (as in being employed as a political correspondent) or specifically (as in being sent to interview a particular person). What they write may be modified, often quite drastically, by the editor, or by sub-editors employed for that very purpose. These changes depersonalize the writing process. The 19th-century convention of the anonymity of journalists (which survived into the second half of the 20th century on some newspapers and magazines) was rooted in a realistic recognition of this relationship. The story 'by' a particular journalist is often merely based on that journalist's reports. These are edited for length, style and content by a sub-editor and perhaps again by the editor; they are introduced by a headline also written by the sub-editor or editor, which may itself give a particular bias to the reader's perception of the story. The journalist's original version may even be augmented by additional information from other sources. Not all journalists, or indeed editors, work in this way. Some are self-employed and, like some writers of books, are commissioned to write particular articles on specific topics, or perhaps to contribute a regular feature or column. Editorial control is still there, but the relationship is perhaps a more equal one.

Even the most cursory consideration of how writers work in the newspaper and magazine industries reveals very starkly the commercial basis of the author-publisher relationship, and consequently the importance of that commercial relationship in the process of information transfer. The great variety of forms of printed publication means that there are many different manifestations of this relationship, but there is, on closer analysis, little fundamental difference between them. An author who wants to communicate with a reader can usually only do so if there is a publisher willing and able to facilitate this. At the heart of the creative process of writing lies a commercial transaction without which the results of the author's creativity cannot be shared with the reader.

The role of the publisher is central in the information market-place because it is the publisher whose risk capital allows it to operate. In book publishing, the editor is the *de facto* gatekeeper at the entrance to the market. The publisher's editor has a very different role from the newspaper editor, although they are both employed by the publisher to act as arbiters of what is produced in the publisher's name. The primary role of the publisher's editor is to select material for publication, although this process is by no means as passive as that statement might imply. Again, a simple model is a useful starting-point. In such a model, an author writes a book and sends it speculatively to a publisher; it is read by an editor, accepted and published. That model might itself be an interesting subject for a novel for it is indeed little more than a work of fiction. A handful of books, mainly first novels, do reach print in this way. Publishers are bombarded with such works from unknown authors. Some of them are read; a very few (estimates vary, but hover at around 1% of those submitted) are accepted and published. It is one way to break into print, but it is neither the most common nor the most effective.

Most authors of books have previous experience as writers, whether as journalists, magazine contributors or academics. Virtually all non-fiction is commissioned from an author before it is written, on the basis of a synopsis which has often been developed jointly between author and editor. Many authors, and probably all who depend on writing as their main source of income, use literary agents to negotiate with publishers and others on their behalf. The author who knows that the book will be published has to work within the constraints of the market-place in fulfilling a contractual obligation to the publisher. These constraints are manifold. A typical contract specifies the subject of the book (usually in the form of a working title), its approximate length, when it is to be delivered to the publisher and in what form. In return the author normally receives a sum of money on signature of contract, and a further sum on delivery and acceptance of the work; thereafter, authors are paid a percentage (usually between 10% and 12.5%) of the receipts from the sale of the book, known as a royalty.

The contract is itself determined by the operation of the information market-place. The subject, and perhaps the author, of the book are its principal selling point, and the publisher's willingness to take on a particular title rests ultimately on an estimate of its marketability. There are some data which can be used as a guide. Typically, about 10% of the annual output of British and American publishers is of works of fiction and a further 8% or 9% consists of children's books; the remaining 80% or so is spread across the whole range of non-fiction. History and biography are by far the most popular categories, with science, medicine, sociology, business books and computing not far behind, but none of these account for more than 5% of the output, and typically they are between 3% and 4%. This is critical to the book publisher's under-standing of the information market-place: it is very diverse.

The diversity of publishing

Few publishers try to work across the whole range of subjects and levels of books. In the larger companies which dominate the global English-language publishing industry, specialist editors are normally responsible for different parts of the list. The basic division is between fiction and non-fiction, although both of these are usually further subdivided. In trade jargon, fiction is divided between 'literary' and 'popular', although even fiction editors sometimes have difficulty in explaining the difference between them. The implication is that it is qualitative. A cynical, but not entirely unrealistic, definition might be to regard popular fiction as fiction which sells and literary fiction as fiction which does not; but this is too crude, and disguises genuine differences. Under the 'popular' umbrella there are many different genres, often used by publishers, librarians and readers to define their own interests: these are such categories as 'science fiction', 'thrillers', 'romances', 'historical novels', and so on.

Non-fiction is, perhaps surprisingly, even less easy to categorize. Many publishing houses specialize in particular subject areas, such as law, medicine or business books. Others cover a wider range, and it is in such firms that specialist editors are typically employed. A distinction which is normally made is between non-fiction for the specialist and non-fiction for the general reader, although there is some overlap. The former is usually known as 'academic' or 'STM' (scientific-technical-medical) publishing, and the latter as 'trade' or 'general trade' non-fiction. These distinctions are essentially market-driven. Academic or STM books are aimed at a small but easily definable market, which is international, especially for books written in English, and is very largely institutional. Trade non-fiction, on the other hand, is intended to have a wider appeal: it is more often seen in bookshops (although the library market is still of great importance), reviewed in newspapers, recorded in bestseller lists and, in some cases, reprinted in paperback. An author's ability to reach the right audience is effectively determined by the right choice of publisher, and the publisher's understanding of the market for that particular book. That, in turn, depends on the editor.

The precise nature of the editorial role in a publishing house varies according to what is being published, and perhaps the traditions and customs of the firm, but any good editor is an active participant in the publishing process. Above all, the editor is a recruiter of authors, often from among those whose reputation has been established in other ways. The pool for non-fiction includes journalists and other professional writers, as well as academics. It is an essential part of editors' jobs to keep abreast of the fields with which they are concerned. This is done partly through market research, usually in the form of statistical data published regularly by the Publishers' Association and the Association of American Publishers, various official and semi-official agencies such as the Central Statistical Office and the Library and Information Statistics Unit, trade journals such as *The Bookseller* and *Publishers' Weekly*, and independent market surveys such as those in *Euromonitor*. Even more important, however, is the development and exploitation of a network of contacts built up over many years in the trade, in the literary and academic worlds and among journalists and other opinion-makers. This is the invisible college of publishing; a working knowledge of it is the core of the editor's expertise. This knowledge is a valuable if ill-defined commodity, which editors can take from job to job, sometimes complete with the authors whose careers they have helped to develop.

The importance of the editorial role becomes even greater when the end-product is more complex. For a multi-authored work, or for major works of reference, the publishing house is a party to many different contractual obligations, all of which have to be brought to fruition at the right moment and in the right order if the book is to be successful. The publisher's editor and the authors or editors of such works collaborate closely as a team, further diluting the concept of authors and publishers as separate and even conflicting entities.

The editor's job does not end when the book is written. Before the book can reach the bookshops it needs to go through a whole series of operations. Traditionally, the work was read by an expert in the field, or a person of literary judgement, before it was finally accepted. This form of quality control, however, is alleged not to be as stringent as used to be the case. The sheer quantity of material which crosses an editor's desk and the need to work quickly in order to maximize the immediate financial returns on a book have partly eliminated it. So too has modern technology. When an author submits work on a disk, as is now normal, there are both economic and technical motives for treating that as an authoritative file. There are always financial pressures on the editor. A publisher gets no return on the investment in a title until it is available for sale; from receipt of text from the author to the first sales rarely takes less than six months. During all of that time, the publisher is spending more money: the author has already been partly paid; editors have to be paid; the book has to be printed and bound; and most of the costs of advertising and marketing are incurred. Speed is paramount, for large and small publishers alike, so that the book can begin to earn its living.

The concern of the editor, therefore, is to put the book into a saleable form as quickly as possible. It is edited, for style and spelling if not for content, designed and then sent for typesetting. If this is not done from disks supplied by the author, the text will also have to be proofread once each by the typesetter (although this is increasingly unusual) and by the publisher, and normally by the author as well. This introduces further costs and delays and is the fundamental reason why publishers now normally demand electronic submission. In any case, authors expect to see proofs, and indeed there may be some additional work to do at this stage, such as the compilation of an index. While all of this is going on, the book is advertised through the trade press, or, in some cases, by direct mailshots to potential customers on the publisher's mailing list, or the mailing list of agencies which the publisher uses. Eventually, when the book is printed, it goes to a warehouse from which it will be distributed either by the publisher itself, or by a distribution agency that it employs. Thirty days after the first copy is sold to a bookseller, the publisher will, at last, get some revenue to set against the very substantial investment which has been made.

This chain of communication from author to reader is informed and determined at every stage by commercial considerations. Quality is important, and few publishers would consciously produce an inferior product. There are, however, no absolute criteria of quality. Novels which would, on literary grounds, be wholly unacceptable to one publisher are the mainstay of another; non-fiction which would not see the light of day from a university press may top the bestseller lists for weeks and be the pride and joy of a general trade publisher. The industry is large enough to be diverse; in this diversity lies both its strength and its weakness.

New directions in publishing

The contemporary practices of traditional publishing have been dealt with at some length because the book publishing process has become the paradigm of information transfer. Even its vocabulary has been carried into new technologies, where there is no hesitation in talking about 'publishing' on the web, or referring to the 'publication' of educational videos or computer software. Indeed some of the products are sold through 'bookshops'. The convergence of technologies, and the gradual displacement of print by other media, has further confused the issue. Databases, held by their creators and accessible online through networks and hosts, are, in the most literal sense, 'published', that is they are made public. Many, however, are by no means in the public domain in the same way that books are, because the commercial basis on which access is achieved is quite different. Buying access to a database, which normally involves purchasing both time and information, is a very different commercial transaction from buying a book. In a library, a reference book bought by the institution instantly becomes a multi-user tool; an online search of a distant database, on the other hand, is conducted by or for an individual user and can, at least in theory, be precisely costed and therefore accurately charged. Although the intellectual processes and editorial procedures in the compilation of a database are, both conceptually and in many functional aspects, analogous to the compilation of a conventional printed reference book, the methods and circumstances of access to the end-product are fundamentally different. The implications of these differences, and the creation of new business models to meet the changed circumstances of information transfer, will be explored in greater detail in Chapter 4.

The use of information technology has led to profound changes in the world of publishing and printed information, as was suggested in Chapter 2. This manifests itself in many ways. Even within the conventional publishing process, as it has been described, the use of computers has put the author in a more powerful and perhaps more responsible position, vis-à-vis the editor. The demand for content to be submitted in electronic form has shifted some aspects of publishing away from the publisher. The concept of 'house style', by which publishers traditionally imposed their own practices of italicization, indentation and other technical features on the text, becomes suddenly less attractive when it involves lengthy and expensive editing of a text which is already internally consistent when it arrives from the author, even if it does not precisely conform to the publisher's own absolute preferences. This is one of those technological paradoxes referred to at the end of Chapter 2; electronic text is in many ways easier to manipulate than text on paper, but the potential problems of doing so often deter the editor from intervening.

Changes in editorial practices, by no means all of them intentional, are not the only way in which computers have impinged on publishing. Quite apart from straightforward business uses such as are now found in all organizations, computers are used throughout the printing industry, where they displaced traditional typesetting methods in the 1980s and also control much of the printing machinery. They are also integral to book ordering and distribution systems. Bibliographic databases, often compiled at national level, are as important in the book trade as they are to librarians, and the International Standard Book Number (ISBN), with its associated bar-code, was developed as a unique identifier of a book in the trade before it was adopted by libraries.

Internet bookselling is only the most public manifestation of change. Direct ordering and payment online by the end-user is having an impact on traditional bookshops; by 2007, Amazon.co.uk was the third largest British bookseller, although still with less than one-third of the value of sales of the next largest, W. H. Smith. Small businesses are losing trade, and the big booksellers are themselves competing in cyberspace by developing their own e-commerce facilities for private customers. After 30 years of experimentation and innovation (and a few failures), the perspective is now long enough for us to see that the use of computers has almost certainly been a factor in holding book prices at a reasonable level and keeping the increases in prices roughly in line with the general rate of price inflation.

These changes have been important, but even more important changes are taking place in those areas of the market where information technology has done more than merely change the means by which books are written, edited, printed and distributed. In some fields of publishing, the use of computers has facilitated wholly new developments whose products are displacing the printed book itself. These developments have involved the creation of information media which, while retaining much of the ease of use of the book, can also overcome some of its inherent disadvantages The printed book is, in many ways, a remarkably flexible medium. It is portable, easily stored, familiar, user-friendly and adaptable to many purposes. It does, however, have two major limitations: it is impossible to change, and it can only be consulted in an essentially linear mode. Both of these points deserve further explanation.

Once a book has been printed, it cannot be altered except by reprinting from a new, or amended, setting of the type or its computer-generated equivalent. This process is both time-consuming and expensive, and runs up against the basic economics of book production. Typically, books are printed in editions ('print runs' in book trade parlance) of between a few hundred and many tens of thousands, but most often between 1500 and

5000 copies. This gives access to some of the economies of scale which characterize mass production processes in other industries, but by no means to all of them. The inhibiting factor lies in the size, or rather the smallness, of the print run itself. A modern printing press can print 1500 copies of a sheet in far less than one hour; a typical book contains no more than between 10 and 15 sheets, each folded to make 16 or 32 pages. In theory, a print run of 1500 copies of a book can be completed in a working day. In practice, however, the whole process is delayed by what happens between sheets, when the metal plate from which the printed impression is actually made has to be removed from the press and the plate for the next sheet substituted for it. This down time (known traditionally as 'make-ready' time) adds significantly to the delays and costs of printing. The shorter the print run, the larger the proportion of down time during the printing process, inevitably increasing the costs.

Because of this basic technical consideration, print runs of less than about 500 are almost never economic using traditional, non-digital printing. Even that is acceptable only for specialized books where the market will bear a consequently high price. This traditional obstacle is now being overcome. Using traditional methods and formats, if a book becomes out of date, it can only be updated if it is printed in similar numbers. Sometimes this happens; there are obvious examples of books which are updated at regular intervals (such as *Who's Who* or *Wisden's Cricketers' Almanac*, for example) and of others (such as this one) which are updated at irregular intervals as the need arises. Economically, however, this can only be justified if the market for the new edition is comparable with that for the old one; hence revised editions of annuals or reprints of textbooks used by successive generations of students are economically viable, but for most books they are not. As a result, books are now typically 'in print' (that is available through normal commercial channels) for little more than a year or so, at which point it often makes more sense for a publisher to replace the title by a new one on a similar subject rather than revise an existing title for which most of the market potential has been exhausted. This, however, involves substantial reinvestment. The inflexibility of the text of a printed book, and the need to produce the book itself in substantial quantities, are the major disadvantages of the medium, and never more so than at a time when the quantity of information is increasing, and demand for its currency is insistent.

The second inhibitory factor is inherent in the codex form of the book itself: it is linear. It is, of course, possible to turn to any given page of a book without starting at page 1 and working forward from there. It is indeed the normal practice in almost all non-fiction to provide tables of contents and indexes which are designed to facilitate precisely that method of use. On the other hand, the user is limited in two important ways. First, it is not possible to consult more than one page at the same time, or to bring together information from more than one page, without transferring it to some other medium by, for example, taking notes or making photocopies. Secondly, the use of the various searching devices such as an index is limited by the work of their compilers; the index leads only to the passages chosen by the indexer, even if, in practice, the indexing terms themselves may not represent the interests of a particular user. It is in this sense that the linear nature of the book, inherent in its physical form, makes it so unsatisfactory for some purposes.

The impact of computers

For over 500 years, these limitations were accepted; at first, perhaps this was because the printed book represented such a great advance on its manuscript predecessor, and later simply because of familiarity and inertia. With computers, however, the limitations no longer exist. First, the updating, revision and correction of data can be a continuous process, and the user can have virtually instantaneous access to the updated version. This is precisely what happens in an online database, where additions or corrections can be immediately incorporated into the file without any delay. For the user of a library catalogue, the decrease in delay is convenient; for the user of a financial information service, continuous updating and absolute currency of information are essential. The computer thus overcomes the first of the great limitations of print because it can actually exploit the essential impermanence of an electronic information store. While this has clear and obvious benefits, there are, however, some counterbalancing issues to be considered. The permanence of print meant that it was normally clear when a book or journal paper was published. This is not necessarily true of an electronic publication, so that the concept of 'time-stamping' has been developed. In essence, this is a mechanism which ensures that each version of the database which remains accessible is indelibly associated with a statement of when it was compiled; 'version control' is an essential element of authoritative electronic publishing. With proper control, content is as authoritative as print-on-paper and often more current; without it, the product cannot be properly evaluated.

The consultation of electronic data is not confined by the linear characteristics of the book. A search, making use of an indexing term which is under the effective control of the user, will reveal all uses of the term in the store, and will bring them together on the screen or on successive screens from which they can then, if the user so wishes, be printed out. The search is controlled by the user, not by the indexer. Once the data have been retrieved, they can be processed in many different ways. They may merely be printed, so that they can be filed like a printed document or a photocopy. They can, however, be downloaded into other files, combined with data from other sources, and electronically processed in a way devised by the user. The possibilities are almost limitless.

For some years, the obvious theoretical benefits of computer-held files as against printed books were not fully or adequately exploited. There were some technical reasons for this, as well as inevitable and natural human resistance to change. It was, however, the economic factors which were the greatest inhibitors of change. The money broker does indeed need instant access to information; research scientists, on the other hand, do not, even though they want to minimize the delay. It is no accident that the earliest commercially successful databases were in such fields as finance and law, where it is critically important to have current and accurate information. The cost of instant access to information was very high in the 1970s and early 1980s, even though the technology for it existed. Typically, it was achieved through telecommunications links to host computers in which databases were held.

Both the information itself and the use of the communications systems were valorized. There was a good deal of debate about the valorization of information and the partial commodification of information services which it brought in its wake. The charge for access included both the cost of the information (determined and assigned by the creators and owners of the database) and the cost of the telecommunications (determined by the service provider). It is important to distinguish between the various elements which comprise this charge and form the basis of the commercial transaction. The products of the information industry have been in the commercial domain for over 500 years. In general, however, the price of the product has related to its material production, with the cost of its intellectual content a comparatively less important issue. Typically, no more than about 10% of the total revenue accrued to the creator of the intellectual content, usually an author. The rest of the price represented a return (intended to be profitable) on the publisher's investment in editorial time, business infrastructure, materials and production. When information is taken from databases rather than a printed source, however, it is possible to make a direct charge for each consultation. The system itself can record the identity of the user, the information sought and obtained and the timespan of the search. Charges may accrue for communications time, and for the data retrieved. In other words, commodification has been devolved from the product itself to its content and the means of accessing content.

This is a critical shift in the structure of the information marketplace. The printed book was essentially a common-user item, a good acquired by purchase and thereafter available freely to all who had access to it. Historically, where such access has been through libraries, it has been uncharged at the point and time of consultation. Accessing a database is quite different. The information intermediary does not acquire the database itself, but the right to use it; this is true whether consultation is online or uses some offline medium such as CD. The creator and owner of the database cannot, therefore, recoup the costs of compilation and production by the sale of a product. What is sold is a service. This is fundamentally different from the traditional charge for an information product. The charge, like the information which is provided, is tailored to the precise needs of the recipient. This concept is explored in more detail in Chapter 5.

Until the very end of the last century, long and complex searches attracted very high communications costs, especially for European users, who were often searching databases held in the USA and working from countries where the cost of telecommunications was high by American standards. Moreover, some of the theoretical advantages of online searching of databases could not be fully exploited because it was economically necessary to use skilled intermediaries (usually librarians) in order to minimize the cost by keeping control of expensive connections times. End-users were thus distanced from the information-seeking process, and that process was not fully informed by their specialist subject knowledge. Out of this, there developed a new branch of the information profession itself, in which brokers operated on behalf of clients, searching databases to meet their information needs, providing either on-demand services or a continuous service of provision of relevant information. The brokerage was another value-added element in the transaction, and perhaps completed the absorption of certain kinds of information provision into the sphere of commerce.

The early years of the commercial development and exploitation of online databases starkly illuminated the financial dimension of the information market-place. The demand was there, but many potential customers did not have sufficient resources to buy the product. Inevitably, a new product was developed which would bring supply and demand into balance within the financial scope of the customers. This was the CD-ROM, which has all the advantages, except one, of the online database: it can be searched freely, downloaded without difficulty, and, with appropriate software, is easy to use even for the untrained or inexperienced user. What it lacked was currency, for a CD-ROM, like a book, cannot be updated once it has been made. On the other hand, the files which are reproduced on it can, and because the actual process of producing the disc is both cheap and simple (and economic in far shorter production runs than is the case with printed books), a new disc can be produced at regular intervals (usually of between three and twelve months) to ensure that, for all practical purposes, the database is as current as most ordinary users will ever need. Whatever disadvantages this may entail are more than counterbalanced by the fact that there are no charges for access, because, like a book, once the initial purchase has been made, the disc can be used an unlimited number of times by an unlimited number of users, although the publisher retains control of the data and CD-ROMs can be used across local area networks (such as those in a company, or a library) only under licence agreements. Both online and CD-ROM access to a database are merely tools which enable the user to find the information. The decision on which to use is essentially financial rather than technical; where network facilities are available and affordable, direct online consultation is normally preferred. It was no surprise that CD-ROM was such a success when it first became widely available in the late 1980s, or that it made more inroads into the market for printed books than any previous computer-based information medium. There were significant areas of reference book publishing in which CD-ROM all but displaced the printed word: these included indexes, annual bibliographies and many abstracts, some of which were previously available online, and some only in printed form. CD-ROM was the ideal compromise, for it does well what the printed book did badly, and it did cheaply what an online system does expensively.

The use of optical discs brought the publishing industry closer than ever to the information technology industry. Competition was inevitable, but so was co-operation, for publishers themselves recognized the need to adapt to new and more economic technologies that users actually want. Indeed, unlike many previous non-book formats, the CD-ROM market came to be largely dominated by familiar names from the publishing world, for their editorial expertise and market experience can be directly translated from the older to the newer medium.

The long-term goal, however, continued to be full electronic publication, in which the generation, editing, storage and distribution of content was wholly digital. The testing-ground for electronic publication was the academic research sector. There was a number of reasons for this. Firstly, it might be supposed that researchers operating at the leading edge of their disciplines are inherently interested in innovation; some certainly were, although there was also a good deal of conservatism in the early years. Secondly, in universities and research institutes in all the industrialized countries, network access was a *de facto* free good at the point of use, just as libraries had been. Individual researchers in universities were not charged for network access; their institutions typically paid annual fees for unlimited usage. Thirdly, there were sound economic reasons for trying to break the publishers' monopoly on the dissemination of research outcomes, which was becoming increasingly burdensome by the end of the 20th century. We shall return to this in Chapter 4.

The interdependent media: convergence and change

Technological developments and economic necessity have been the driving forces behind important changes in the chain of information transfer from author to reader, or from creator to user. Some traditional media have been changed; others have been wholly or partly displaced. The result is greater diversity, in which the wider range of choice allows the producer and the user to determine the most suitable medium for a particular purpose. This is not a purely technological issue. Media do not succeed simply because they work: they are successful because customers find them useful, in the sense that they can do things for them that they want, at prices that they (or their information providers) can afford. This is not the only way in which consumer choice has determined how information media have changed. An equally striking and more generally applicable example is to be found in the newspaper industry.

Throughout the industrialized world, most people now obtain whatever knowledge they have of current affairs from television and radio and, increasingly, from the internet. Almost all general broadcasting services have news bulletins of some sort, although the more specialized satellite and cable services do not. These broadcasters typically make use of either correspondents or agencies which allow them to give virtually instantaneous access to the news as it breaks. News channels, such as Cable News Network (CNN) and BBC News 24, have, despite initially gloomy forecasts, proved to be a great success, and the demand for such channels, both on radio and on television, is clearly real. There is no doubt that the interest in the news is both widespread and genuine. At the same time, the circulation of newspapers has fallen dramatically during the last 30 years. We do not have to look far for the reason. Broadcast and online news is both easier to absorb and cheaper to receive than printed news; it is also more current and its impact more immediate. The very demise of the newspaper has been forecast more than once, and, indeed, many have closed down; yet many remain, and many of them are very successful. But new challenges continue to develop. The major broadcasters now put their news bulletins on their websites either in real time as a simultaneous broadcast and webcast, or subsequently as a podcast or in an archive. The latter in particular give consumers a new power: in effect, they can access a bulletin at a time convenient to them rather than to the broadcaster. Some newspapers have responded by doing the same thing; despite the space available, especially in the broadsheets, there is not room for everything that they would like to publish, and the web-based versions can give more in-depth accounts, complete transcripts of interviews of which only part is published in the printed version, and so on. The survival of the newspaper as a mass medium has been achieved by adaptation to changed circumstances. In both Britain and the USA, this evolutionary development has had two dimensions. At one end of the market, the 'serious' press has increasingly taken on the characteristics of a news magazine. There is still much reporting of 'hard' news in the broadsheets, with back-up from even more detailed reports on the newspaper's website. There is also a great deal of comment, interpretation, analysis and background, as well as features on a wide range of topics from science to fashion. At the other (and more profitable) end of the market, news reporting in the traditional sense has almost vanished; politics is dealt with largely at the level of abuse, personal interest stories and covert or overt commentary, while much of the 'news' in the tabloids is actually about such matters as television soap operas (and their stars), the private lives of famous people, and the like. The development of free newspapers (delivered to the home or available at supermarkets) merely reiterates the relative unimportance of news at the popular end of the spectrum. These free-sheets are financed entirely from advertising revenue.

In fact, the broadsheets, the tabloids and the free-sheets are all trying to address the same set of issues, and are working from similar assumptions: they are finding ways to survive as *news*papers in a society in which they are not the preferred *news* medium. They have done so by changing the definition of news. Much of what is written in the broadsheets actually assumes a basic factual knowledge of persons and events, knowledge which has been acquired through the broadcast and electronic media.

Because they cannot compete in immediacy, they compete in depth and in detail; they report what radio and television cannot report because of the time limitations on their broadcasts. The tabloids also assume that their readers are familiar with the subjects of their articles, whether these are celebrity footballers or actors in the soaps. This has had further consequences. The changes in the broadsheet newspapers have been a factor in driving some British weeklies out of business, for the newspapers now perform the function formerly unique to them, and indeed in preventing the development of American-style news magazines (such as *Time* and *Newsweek*) in Britain, because they already fulfil much of their potential role. The tabloids have had a similar effect on different magazines. In other words, the news market, like the very different market for papers in scientific journals, has been changed under consumer pressure. Consumers turn to the broadcast media for instant news, to the print media for analysis, detail and diversity and then to the newspaper's websites for an even deeper layer of detail. The survival of the newspaper has been made possible by the publishers' recognition of the changed circumstances in the information market-place.

The interrelated and interdependent roles of different media and technologies are being redefined by economic and cultural factors, and by the perceptions and wishes of their customers and audiences. The market-place is growing and fragmenting simultaneously. Technologies as well as suppliers are in competition with each other, and there is only limited space for successful operations. The changing nature of newspapers and the development of electronic scientific journals are only two examples of the results of this process. Underlying all of this change is the changing structure of the communications industry, which, like its technology, is increasingly global rather than national, with all the implications of such universality for the countries in which it operates. Even such a comparatively parochial dimension of the industry as British publishing illustrates this point.

UK publishers sold products to the value of some £2.8 billion in 2005. This was a continuing upward trend as it had been for many years, often in excess of the rate of inflation; in other words, there was typically real growth. In the USA, the market in 2006 was worth about $24.2 billion. In both countries, and throughout the global market of English-language works, the market was dominated by a few major groups, each of them embracing a wide range of activities in both book publishing and other media. All of them had a significant global presence, and all were also involved in other media.

HarperCollins, one of the largest of these book publishing groups, is actually only one part of one of the world's dominant media conglomerates, News Corp. This massive company (its revenue in the fiscal year 2006 was US $3.4 billion) dominates in several key information and communication markets. HarperCollins in its present manifestation was formed in the early 1980s, when Rupert Murdoch, the Australian media magnate, took over two prestigious but ailing publishing houses, Harper & Row in the USA, and Collins in Britain. They were different but complementary. Harper & Row was an academic and professional publisher, with a long history of respectability in that field. Collins was no less respectable, but had built its reputation on middlebrow fiction, popular religious books and the semi-popular non-fiction in its Fontana list. It was a good combination, but under the Murdoch umbrella HarperCollins is no more than part of the publishing arm of News Corp, whose newspaper interests include *The Times*, *The Sun* and *The Sunday Times*, as well as Australian papers and the *New York Daily News* among nearly 200 titles worldwide. Murdoch's other involvements in the communications industry include BSkyB, the only significant satellite broadcaster in the UK market, and Fox Television, which has a growing presence in the television market (especially among young adults in the USA), and is a major player in video and DVD because of its inherited rights in thousands of popular movies produced by 20th-Century Fox including, for example, the *Star Wars* series. News Corp's interests extend to social networking websites (including MySpace) and other interactive services. The various parts of HarperCollins have been able to defend their editorial independence under this regime, but they are inevitably subject to more stringent financial disciplines. Being a part of one of the world's largest companies is very different from being a small or historic family publishing house.

Two other companies also illustrate the international and multimedia dimension of the information industry. Reed Elsevier came together in its present form in the last decade of the 20th century when the long established Dutch publishing house of Elsevier was consciously pursuing a policy of developing a global presence in scientific publishing, and merged with the British company Reed International. Reed International, which had originally been a papermaking company, was formed in 1970, and came to include many British and foreign publishers, including Heinemann, Methuen, Philips and Octopus in Britain, R. R. Bowker in the USA, K. G. Saur in Germany, and other interests in Australia. Elsevier, which can trace its origins back to the 17th century, was primarily publishing scientific and academic books and journals, and had moved quickly into electronic publishing within its fields. Reed Elsevier's interests include magazines, British regional newspapers, scholarly and scientific journals, satellite broadcasting, online information services and CD-ROM publishing. It acquires and disposes of subsidiaries at an almost bewildering speed for purely commercial reasons.

Another great cross-media company is Pearson, which includes in its portfolio newspapers, magazines and books, as well as both terrestrial and satellite television. Its newspapers include *The Financial Times*, while its book publishing interests encompass the 250-year-old Longman empire, one of the great monuments of British publishing, and Penguin Books, among other less famous imprints.

Perhaps the most interesting example of all is Time-Warner. Time-Warner came together from the worlds of magazine and book publishing on the one hand and the cinema on the other. The company which had been *Time* magazine diversified by expansion and acquisition across the whole range of print publishing. In due course it amalgamated with the company which had begun as Warner Brothers. Warner was one of the great production and distribution giants of the golden age of Hollywood from the 1930s to the early 1960s. It continued to flourish, not least because of its control of thousands of movies which were still in demand; a new generation of fans was buying them on video, and the appetite of the ever-increasing number of television stations for old movies was seemingly insatiable. When Time-Warner came into existence it was a formidable player. It became all the more formidable when it merged with America On-Line (AOL), the first, and still the largest, commercial internet service provider (ISP). Other interests include cable television, Home Box Office, movie production (through both Warner Brothers and other parts of the group) and music production. AOL-Time-Warner is a powerful symbol of convergence and of the ever-growing importance of the internet as a medium of communication for all purposes. At a time when communications have never been more important, the world's media are increasingly under the control of a small number of companies and individuals.

Not all of these multinational media conglomerates have their origin in the English-speaking world. The German group Bertelsmann has a significant part in both publishing and the broadcast media. Bertelsmann, among many other interests, includes in its portfolio the publisher Random House, acquired in 1998 and at that time the largest single publisher in the UK market. The company is also heavily involved, through some of its other imprints, in academic and STM publishing, and in publishing educational books. Random House itself was the result of a series of mergers and takeovers in the American and British publishing industries. Bertelsmann's interests range across the whole spectrum of the information and communications industries from print publishing to internet content creation and management, and television production and networks.

Even from these brief accounts, it is clear that the competition between media is being conducted at least partly in the context of competition *within* companies. These global companies exist in a world of global communications and information systems which are technologically independent of political boundaries, and as corporations they themselves do not have a significant national identity. They are essentially supranational bodies. Their very existence raises important political questions about the regulatory regimes under which their different parts operate in different countries. Almost all of the book and newspaper publishing activities of these groups take place under conditions which can loosely be described as being a 'free' press, but broadcasting and telecommunications regimes vary widely. One consequence is that, on the one hand, companies have to be aware of and conform to many different standards, and, on the other, they are able to do things in one market which would be illegal in another where they also operate. Some of the political and social implications of these issues will be pursued in Chapter 6.

The market: definition and size

The market in which publishing companies operate is one that is fairly well understood, although some other aspects of the information market have been less thoroughly described and analysed. In 2005, (the most recent year for which data is publicly available at the time of writing), some 206,000 new titles or revised editions were published in the UK; in 2002, there had been 125,000. The total has more than doubled in a decade (in 1996 it was 101,000). But this growth is typically more of the same; for many years, the largest single category of new books has been fiction, at between 9 and 10% of total output. The equivalent data from the USA is in terms of revenues rather than titles, but it shows a similar pattern of growth, with a 10% increase in sales from 2004 to 2005, well ahead of the rate of price inflation. In other words, print-on-paper publishing of books is expanding, not contracting, despite competing formats and media.

These figures help us to define some of the most important characteristics of this sector of the information market-place. First, it deals with a very large number of what marketing experts call 'product lines'. The 206,000 British editions were, of course, joining many of those published in 2004, and some of those published in 2003, as well as smaller numbers from earlier years; and also books imported from abroad, especially the USA, for which the UK is part of a global export market for books. Since, in practice, few retail bookshops in Britain carry a stock of more than about 20,000 titles, there is much competition for a place on their shelves, and hence for the attention of potential book-buyers. Of course, not all books are sold through bookshops, but some 70% of all sales by value in 2002 were to individual consumers, as against 30% to public and private sector institutions. As a market of over £2.6 billion, the consumer book market is one worth fighting for. It is also a market which is wide open for e-commerce; the diversity of products, the comparatively small market for almost all of them, and the typically high-end socio-economic and educational profiles of purchasers all favour this development, as the success of Amazon and others have dramatically demonstrated.

Even these figures pale into comparative insignificance beside the circulation figures of newspapers and magazines. The mass circulation

British tabloids regularly attract daily sales of more than three million copies, and the most popular of the British broadsheets, *The Daily Telegraph*, sells nearly a million. In this context, the sales of books are small indeed, although newspaper sales have continued to fall since the late 1990s while book sales have increased. The British magazine market is also of great commercial importance and commands a large market. The most popular magazines for women sell about 500,000 as do those aimed at the youth market. Some TV guide magazines and a few others sell more than one million. All of this, however, must be put into the context of the most popular mass medium of all. Television must attract millions of viewers to survive, especially in the case of the vast majority of channels that have no public subsidy or other non-commercial sources of revenue. The market has, however, fragmented in recent years. Where viewing figures in millions were once commonplace for the most popular programmes, the multiplication of channels has reduced the domination of the traditional terrestrial broadcasters. Where once episodes of soap operas such as *Coronation Street* or *EastEnders* could attract audiences of more than ten million, or over 20% of the adult population, several times a week throughout the year, such exposure is now rarely achieved, and then usually by major sporting events rather than by specially created content.

Although television is a distinctive sector of the information market-place, it is related to the market for the printed word and for other information media. As we have seen in looking at how newspapers have changed, different parts of the media influence each other, and to some extent sustain and boost each other. The tabloid press is essentially part of the entertainment industry and reflects that in its choice of content and style of presentation. The celebrities who feature in the tabloids, and in many popular magazines, are often seen on television or on the sports field. The cult of celebrity is a significant commercial factor in the mass media in early 21st-century Britain. Despite this, in broad terms, the reading of books has remained constant, but it is certainly not comparable with television viewing. Surveys over the last 20 years have fairly consistently produced the same results; while 99% of the adult British population watch television at some time during the week, fewer than 50% read a book. Moreover, while television viewing is similar across socio-economic divides, book reading

falls below 40% in social groups 4 and 5, rising to more than 65% in groups
1 and 2. The consumer book market has a clear socio-economic bias
towards the wealthier and better educated members of society, whereas
television (in general terms, although not necessarily in terms of specific
choices of viewing) transcends those boundaries. At the same time,
television viewing habits are themselves changing. Multi-channel television,
which is now found in well over 50% of British homes, has led to
fragmentation of the audience. At one end of the scale, the mass-market
terrestrial channels (primarily BBC1 and ITV) can still occasionally attract
ten million or more viewers for individual programmes; at the opposite
extreme, small specialist channels (such as Sky Arts or Men and Motors)
probably number their viewers in a few thousands.

The publishing sector is, as we have seen, increasingly embedded in the
information industry as a whole. This is partly because of the patterns of
ownership which have brought most of the major British and American
commercial publishers into global media and communications conglomerates. But underlying that commercial trend are the driving forces of
convergent technologies and changing customer expectations and behav-
iour. The whole industry has become more competitive. In the information
market, print publishing's competitors now include CD-ROMs, online
digital resources and the world wide web. In the leisure market, books are
in competition with newspapers and magazines among print products, as
well as multi-channel television and other electronic media, not to mention
all the other competing claims on leisure time from sport to gardening.

As we have seen, the printed word has already been superseded in
some parts of the information market-place. The high-value, high-cost end
of the market is in the provision of databases, abstracts and other value-
added service. But this is trivial in size compared with the ever-increasing
number of organizations, institutions and companies with their own sites
on the world wide web. The development of the web can already be seen
as one of the key episodes in the history of the internet. Although it began
in the scientific community, its inventor, Tim Berners-Lee, deliberately
released it into public domain as a platform for a genuinely user-friendly,
interactive, hypermedia information system. Its success has been
phenomenal. It is the principal reason why a networked PC has become

as common as the telephone and the television set in many households in developed countries. In June 2007, some 1.17 billion people in the world (about 17% of the total population) accessed the internet; this represented an increase of 225% since the year 2000. But widescale usage and mass access are concentrated in a comparatively small number of countries; some 210 million of users in June 2007 were in the USA, 86 million in Japan, 50 million in Germany and 37 million in the United Kingdom. Well over 500 million people around the world live in households with internet access. In October 2006, *The Financial Times* reported that for the first time people were spending more time on the web than in reading newspapers. This is a global market unique in history. Unconstrained by national boundaries, and with very light legal and regulatory constraints, the internet has become the information medium with truly global content. We shall return to some of the implications of this throughout the remaining chapters of this book.

The provision of electronic information into the home is not entirely confined to the use of the internet. Most domestic televisions have, for the last 20 years, had a teletext facility, through which they can receive the broadcast digital signals of such services as ORACLE and CEEFAX. These are now entirely digital, and have become more user-friendly than their analogue predecessors. Although the user is confined by the provider's decisions about what content should be available, relative ease of navigation and the currency of the information makes digital teletext an attractive medium for some purposes. For the user who (typically) is looking for local or regional weather or travel information, teletext provides relatively easy access to information which is otherwise available only at some expense (perhaps by telephone, either by voice or as data on a website), intermittently (when it is broadcast at the whim of the broadcasters), or not at all.

Despite the growth of the web, teletext services still have some importance. Locally based services, some funded by advertising revenue, and others supported by local authorities or public-private sector joint ventures, are beginning to become more familiar. Unlike the national services, they tend to be in public places rather than in the home, providing, for example, information about local public transport services, environmental and planning information, or the sort of information and advice traditionally available from a Citizens Advice Bureau, a tourist information centre or a public library. Terminals are sometimes accessible to the public, or sometimes used by intermediaries; in either case, they represent another electronic incursion into the formerly protected world of print, and another electronic extension of access to information. Both public providers and the broadcasting organizations link teletext services with their websites, often using them as a summary of, or introduction to, the more detailed information that is provided on the web. For the broadcasters, the development of more sophisticated web-linked teletext services is part of their exploitation of digital technologies, which also includes the development of limited interactive facilities (for example, to give the viewer some choice between camera angles in watching a football match) and the use of the digital network for other purposes, such as e-mail.

The convergence of information and communication technologies lies at the heart of all these changes and developments. The creation of what was called an 'information superhighway', a common-carrier network for digital signals, was on the political agenda in the early 1990s in both Europe and the USA. The predictions and expectations about how this would be achieved have proved to be somewhat inaccurate in detail, but nevertheless the superhighway has been created. The original assumption was that the basis of the development would be cable with a wide bandwidth that would allow rapid transmission of voice and multimedia digital data with full interactive capacity. In fact, the initial take-up of broadband, particularly in Europe, was slow, but it did gradually have an impact by giving better and faster access. Existing telecommunications networks were redeveloped as digital broadband. Perhaps even more importantly, wireless networks for mobile telephony also developed broadband capacity (after a somewhat stuttering start because of the high capital costs of infrastructure development) and began to create an environment in which users had *de facto* unlimited access regardless of where they were. Although we no longer use the terminology, it is the superhighway which has opened up e-banking, e-shopping and e-government. The development of e-commerce, the first boom of the 21st century, is an established fact; in 1995 it was all but unknown. In the last five years of the old century, the internet took a firm hold on the domestic market in all the industrialized countries. Activities from shopping for groceries to trading stocks and shares moved into the cyberspace. A whole new sector – the so-called 'dotcom' sector – was added to the developed economies. The collapse of the dotcom bubble as a stock market phenomenon should not be allowed to disguise the fact that there has been massive change. Broadcasters, newspaper editors, advertisers, service providers, charities and governments all refer us to their websites to learn more, to buy and to trade. The ubiquitous URL is the symbol of the revolution.

Fragmentation or competition?

The fragmentation of the information market-place is, it seems, a necessary condition of this expansion and continuing growth. Within living memory, it consisted of little more than the printed word. It now contains a multitude of competing and complementary sectors. Although print continues to predominate in some of these, in others it is supplemented and in some it has been replaced. Others again are completely new; they are sectors into which the printed word never went and indeed could never go. Competition has introduced a sharper edge to the commercial element which has always been intrinsic in the process of information transfer. The new technologies all need massive investments, but they are developing so quickly that the investment is likely to be of comparatively short-term value. The replacement of computer systems on a four-year cycle is well established throughout the industrialized world, but we are now also seeing the cyclical replacement of some parts of the infrastructure as well, with the development of new communications systems based on geostationary satellites and fibre optic cabling. The experience of the last 20 years suggests that the pace of change and of technological development will certainly not diminish and will probably increase.

The overtly competitive element has raised a whole range of issues which were formerly suppressed even when they were identified. Information has never been 'free', but now it can be realistically costed. To some extent this has always been possible; for example, the data which are now used to define the cost of each loan made by a public library have always been available, but methodologies for making use of them were only developed when the political and economic climate demanded that the information be obtained and used. Similar calculations can be made about almost any information transaction, with greater or lesser difficulty, and greater or lesser significance. Where realistic and meaningful costings of the transaction are possible, the temptation to pass them on to the end-user is often irresistible and may become mandatory. The new competitors in the information market-place do not share, or perhaps even understand, the benevolent desire to inform which is the common heritage of the traditional information providers, the librarians. Publishers have always known the cost of information, but even they disguised it to some extent, and only in the harsher climate of multinational corporations has publishing had to become the hard-edged business which it must now be to survive. Yet the greatest expansion of all is on the world wide web, the ultimate in 'free' access to information. Some of these issues and their implications are among the subjects of Chapters 4 and 5.

Chapter 4

Access to information

It is comparatively easy to demonstrate that information is not free. A book borrowed from a library may be 'free' to the user at the point at which the service is delivered, but the costs are borne from taxation. There may be a mismatch between taxpayers and borrowers, but in practice every borrower is, in one way or another and with only rare exceptions, an indirect contributor to the cost of both the book and the library. It is possible to calculate the direct cost of each loan, and that piece of information can be used to make a basic calculation about the value for money of the service. Financial calculations, however, are only the beginning. What is far more difficult to assess is *value*. In part, the problem is that such an assessment has to deal with a negative, the thorny problem of the loss which may be incurred by the absence of information. This can probably never be more than an approximation, but information providers who operate successfully in the more competitive parts of the market-place have long since realized that they can charge very high prices to those for whom the lack of information is a matter of concern. The user who needs instantaneous financial data will not query their cost until it manifestly exceeds the losses which would be incurred by not having access to them. It is on this assumption that much of the commercial information industry has been built.

The underlying cultural change is not so much in the solution of such conundrums, but rather in the articulation of them. The development of new information technologies and information delivery systems has fundamentally changed the relationship between the supplier and consumer of information, and the role of the intermediary who comes between them. The traditional model distanced the consumer of information from the cost of providing it, even if it was the consumer who indirectly bore the cost. Moreover, there was an assumption, sometimes unexpressed, that the provision of information, especially in the form of books, was inherently desirable, and the role of the state or of other agencies was to facilitate rather than inhibit the information transfer process. In other words, information was treated as a public good. Historically, this can be illustrated in two examples which are still of great contemporary importance.

The price of books and the cost of broadcasts

First, in many industrialized countries there has been, until quite recently, a mechanism which partially regulates the price of books. This can take many forms, but the most familiar model, which operated in the UK for most of the 20th century, is that of setting a minimum price below which a book may not be sold. The Net Book Agreement, in which this was embodied in 1900 and in a slightly revised form in 1957, was designed to achieve two objectives: to sustain the profit margins of the retail booksellers and of the publishers, and to maintain a steady supply of books on a wide variety of subjects. As a matter of historical fact, it was the former consideration which lay behind the creation of the Agreement during the 1890s, but it was the latter which was the basis of the arguments which sought to justify it during the last 40 years of its existence.

The argument in favour of retail price maintenance on books, whether through the Net Book Agreement, or by similar mechanisms which operated in some other countries, was that books are a cultural as well as a commercial commodity, and that it is, therefore, culturally desirable that a wide variety of them should be available at reasonable prices and in many places. This, it is argued, is inherently difficult because of the economics of book publishing, production and distribution, which were discussed briefly in Chapter 3. Profit margins in the book industry are indeed small, probably no more than about 10% for the publisher on an average title, and perhaps as little as 3% gross for each book sold by a retail bookseller. The case was that if there were price competition between booksellers these margins would prove to be inadequate. Bookshops would close, and the publishers be deprived of their only means of laying their wares before the public. Such shops as survived would only be able to sell highly profitable mass-market books, and consequently publishers would no longer be willing to publish the wide range of books of cultural, scientific and educational value which they currently produce.

The surprising thing about this argument is not that it should have been put forward, but that it should have been accepted almost without question. When the Net Book Agreement apparently fell foul of British law in relation to restrictive trade practices, it was 'tried' in the Restrictive Practices Court in 1963, and 'acquitted' on cultural grounds along the lines suggested in the last paragraph. The argument for free market pricing was barely heard at all; when it was, it commanded no sympathy from the Court. Not until the mid-1990s did the Net Book Agreement come to an end, and then it was largely because a few major publishers and entrepreneurial booksellers effectively chose to ignore it. The consequences fell far short of the predicted cultural catastrophe, although there were significant changes in the retail trade. Some of them, however, were only peripherally related to the demise of the Net Book Agreement. The trend with the greatest long-term implications was the move towards retailing over the internet, both by established retail booksellers such as Blackwell, and by new entrants to the trade, of which the best known is Amazon which operates entirely on the web.

The broader significance of the Net Book Agreement, and similar regulatory mechanisms, was that, despite its purely commercial origins, it was consistently defended on the grounds of social utility and cultural desirability. This was not a marketing ploy by the publishers; it was widely and genuinely accepted at all levels of society that the book was a cultural device as well as being the subject of commercial transactions. Strangely, this argument was not applied to newspapers or to magazines, even when newspapers were closing under economic pressure and diversity of opinion in the press was being eroded. A not dissimilar argument, however, did underlie the organization of broadcasting in the UK from the 1920s to the 1950s, and to some extent still does. Although the BBC was never funded by taxation, the fee for the compulsory licence which provides the bulk of the Corporation's revenue is, in effect, a form of taxation. Listeners (and later viewers) did not pay for what they could afford, but a flat rate set at a level which almost everyone could afford. It is an anomaly which became even more marked after 1955 when programmes transmitted by the BBC's commercial competitors could only be legally received on apparatus which was licensed with money that funded the BBC. Like the defence of the Net Book Agreement, the broadcasting licence fee was ultimately justified on cultural grounds: it provided the basis for a diverse and high-quality public service. Whether or not these arguments (about either bookselling or broadcasting) were justified is, to a large extent, irrelevant. The fact is that they were generally accepted.

To some extent they still are, for the British television licence (it is no longer required for the receipt of radio broadcasting only) still survives. Significantly, however, both were challenged in the 1980s more seriously than ever before in their history. The Net Book Agreement came under attack from within the book trade. It was inimical to the new and more aggressive style of marketing which many booksellers adopted, following the general trend of retailing during that decade. Waterstones, soon to be followed by other, more traditional booksellers like Dillons and W. H. Smith, transformed the public image of the bookshop. Their shops were well lit showcases for books, where customers were welcome to browse and a tolerably competent staff was available to help, to the gentle strains of Vivaldi (also on sale in the CD section) in the background. Terry Maher, one of the pioneers of this new style of bookselling in the Pentos Group (which included Dillons) tried by all means at his disposal to undermine the Net Book Agreement. He initially failed, despite a reference to the Monopolies Commission, an investigation by the Consumers' Association, and unfavourable noises from the European Union about its legislation against anti-competitive practices. Only in 1993 did a government minister take up the theme, and begin to make the apparently obvious link between the abrogation of the Net Book Agreement and the free market economic theories which had dominated British political thought and policy since 1979. The end came in 1997, but by implosion rather than assault. The result has actually been significant growth in book sales, although this has come about largely through the bookselling chains making use of their purchasing power to negotiate deals with publishers which allow them to offer discounts on recommended retail prices and deals, such as 'three books for the price of two'. The small independent bookshops which historically typified the trade have suffered; but book buyers have greatly benefited.

The recent history of the television licence is more political, but no less odd or instructive. The BBC has always proudly maintained a tradition of independence from government, although this has perhaps sometimes worn a little thin when under serious strain at times of national emergency. Broadly speaking, however, there is usually more reality than pretence in this stance, and certainly the Corporation's journalists and reporters have a highly developed talent for annoying politicians just as their colleagues in the printed media do. Unlike print journalists, however, BBC journalists are working for an organization that derives the bulk of its revenue from a form of payment whose level is determined by the government. It is this that puts the BBC in the political firing line.

During the late 1980s and early 1990s, the television industry underwent fundamental change. The franchises to operate the independent terrestrial stations in Britain were redistributed (as they are periodically) on entirely commercial grounds. At the same time, the granting of the first licences for satellite television introduced a new and powerful competitor. The position of an autonomous public service broadcaster supported by a compulsory levy on the owners of television sets, regardless of whether or not they used its services, became even more anomalous. The BBC's Royal Charter, the instrument under which it operates, is renewed decennially. Although the review, which took place in 2004-2005, recommended some significant changes to the governance and public accountability of the BBC, the licence fee itself was retained. Meanwhile, satellite broadcasters became increasingly powerful players (especially in key areas such as live sporting events), the network was being digitized, and a planned programme of turning off analogue signals was agreed, while a number of network providers entered the market. The BBC itself developed a significant digital presence, but many of the ISPs and other companies in the media market were competing for their share of an increasingly fragmented television audience. Fifty years after losing its monopoly of television, the BBC had become one broadcaster among many; it was still a major operator, but it was losing its cultural distinctiveness. Even its proud tradition of news gathering (as opposed to news dissemination) was under threat as it found itself suffering from financial constraints in the first decade of the 21st century.

The history of British broadcasting contrasts strongly with that in the USA. In that country, broadcasting was a private sector activity from the very beginnings of radio, although geographical franchises were awarded by the federal government, and from these there developed networks of programme makers and distributors. Television followed the pattern established by the radio industry in the 1920s and 1930s, although American television from the 1950s to the 1970s was dominated by three major networks (ABC, CBS and NBC). This oligopoly was broken by the development of cable television in the early 1980s, which allowed a far greater number of providers into the market; they ranged from the news service founded by Ted Turner in Atlanta, Georgia, which became CNN, to very localized community-based services. The public service sector – PBS – in the USA was a small latecomer; and it is supported by subscriptions, advertising, sponsorship and donations, not by a quasi-tax.

The political arguments about the funding of the BBC (which no doubt have many years to run) and those about the Net Book Agreement (which are now of historical interest only) have some important similarities. Both are in an arena whose boundaries are being redefined by the diversification and fragmentation of the information market-place. The cultural argument no longer commands universal assent among politicians or voters, or even within the two industries themselves. The non-commercial basis of the funding of a substantial part of the broadcasting industry, like the partial control of book prices, can be argued to be a survival which seems increasingly out of place. The intense competition to supply information and entertainment to consumers is taking place in a commercial ethos in which cultural considerations seem to count for little.

The cost of libraries

The second example of the historic model of the state's generally benevolent attitude towards the information market-place is to be found in public libraries. The public library has become one of the symbols, even perhaps one of the icons, of a 'civilized' society. It is provided, like basic education and social welfare, by using the product of general taxation to fund particular services. The public library pioneers of the 19th century, whether they were philanthropists, well-wishers, political supporters or even librarians, saw public libraries as being for the public good, promoting literacy, education and culture. They became an integral part of the cultural fabric, and were soon to be found in virtually every town and in many villages. Although it was not until 1964 that local authorities in England and Wales were *obliged* to provide a public library service of an acceptable standard, in practice almost all had done so for decades.

What was less often appreciated, and rarely discussed, was that the public libraries are also an integral part of the economic fabric of the book trade. Public libraries in the UK are currently (2006–7) spending about £95 million a year on books, the equivalent of about £2.00 per capita for the population of the UK as a whole. Although expenditure has recovered from a low point in 1997–8, in real terms the long-term trend is a decrease against the price of books, and book expenditure is a decreasing proportion of public library expenditure as a whole. The broader significance of this is two-fold. Firstly, public libraries represent about 5% of the total UK book market, and in some sectors (such as hardback fiction) the public libraries are actually the core market for the publishers. A decrease in the public library market is potentially very damaging to the publishing industry. Secondly, libraries have been quite favourably treated by central and local government since 1997–8, but the bulk of the new money has gone into innovative services rather than traditional provision of books for lending. This reflects not only public demand but also an attempt to make the public library more attractive to a wider audience by effectively turning it into a public point of access to the tools of the information society. In effect, public libraries have become the main channel for public provision of access to networked information services of all sorts.

The involvement of the public libraries in the commercial world of publishing, even if only as customers, always had implications for their role. So too did their tradition of providing services free at the point of delivery. Even in the 1964 Public Libraries Act, this tradition was marginally challenged. Libraries were allowed to charge for certain services to which a cost could be attached, such as borrowing books from other libraries on behalf of users, or providing photocopies. Even more significantly, many libraries began to charge for non-printed media, such as recorded music and, in later years, videos, DVDs, computer software, video games and e-books. Once again, there was an unspoken assumption about the significance, and perhaps even the superiority, of the book. It is unnecessary, for these purposes, to argue whether or not that assumption might have been (or indeed might still be) justified. It is, however, important to notice it, for it was the advent of new media, challenging the book as a tool of entertainment and education, which forced librarians to rethink their attitude to charging their users.

The great majority of librarians, and apparently politicians, still opposes charging for the 'core services' provided by public libraries, and will, no doubt, continue (at least in the case of the librarians) to do so. It is a theme to which we shall return towards the end of this chapter. For the present we need only note that the reopened debate about the funding of the public library service has been impelled, in part, by the implications of the new media of information and communication.

Public good or private profit?

These examples are intended to illustrate two points which they have in common. First, they show the changing relationship between information providers and information consumers. Both sides are aware that their relationship now exists in an overtly commercial context, and in a general economic and political climate in which that context is emphasized. Common-user services, like broadcast television or public libraries, no longer have a monopoly, and can no longer be assumed to be the only paradigms of information delivery or domestic entertainment, any more than the book trade and the publishing industry can continue to assume that they have a uniquely important product. The assignment of costs and value to information itself, as well as to the systems for delivering it, has fundamentally changed our perception of both the product and the service.

Secondly, a consideration of book pricing, public service broadcasting and public library provision illustrates the historically benevolent role of the state in the information transfer process. By permitting a price control regime which was designed to protect certain kinds of culturally or educationally desirable publishing, or supporting a broadcasting organization which had a commitment to high-quality public service programming, the state gave a *de facto* endorsement to those products and services. The provision of services which are free at the point of delivery and which actually compete with charged services (as 'free' public libraries could be argued to compete with booksellers) is an equally remarkable example. It is probable that such benevolent regimes would have changed in any case, but in the last 20 years of the 20th century a combination of political, economic and technological factors made the need to consider change even more urgent.

The political factors varied in their details in different countries, but the overall thrust was similar across the industrialized world. In summary, there was a move away from a centralist model, with a large public sector which was essentially driven by needs and aspirations, towards a more diffused model, with a heavy emphasis on the development of an entrepreneurial private sector which was market-driven. Nowhere was this change more marked than in the UK, where almost 40 years of consensus government (despite shifts between the left and the right) had created a widespread sense of corporatism in the state. The policies which prevailed from 1979 to 1997 led to the return of large parts of the public sector into private hands; for our purposes the most important of these was the telecommunications system, which was privatized in 1984. At the same time, a commitment to competition opened up the market. Again, this was true of telecommunications, where the privatized British Telecom was subject to competition which had not disturbed its nationalized predecessor, just as the BBC and the franchisees of commercial television were subjected to the less controlled competition of the satellite broadcasters. Market-oriented ideologies also formed the theoretical basis of the objections to the Net

Book Agreement, and provided its opponents with some degree of political support.

Electronic communications: access and costs

Political and economic factors thus converged, but even closer was the link between economics and technology. It was during the 1980s that some of the long heralded benefits of the information technology revolution at last began to be felt, as ideas were translated into reality. The computer became a familiar object in the office and the library, and in many homes. It was widely used for a great variety of educational, professional and social purposes, quite apart from the 'hidden' use of computer technology in retailing, manufacturing, transport and many other sectors of the economy. The wider use of computers, however, transformed the parameters of the economic relationship between information providers and information consumers. Simply using computer systems, especially when they were utilized to draw information from distant databases, meant that a cost could be assigned to each individual information transaction. In a library, it is only possible to give an average, and therefore notional, costing of a traditional transaction such as a loan; when information is sought from an online database, however, it is possible to give a precise costing of both the information itself (if it is charged for) and the telecommunications costs. There are still fixed costs for equipment and staff, which have to be added and are as vague as the notional costing of traditional services, but the direct financial transactions which take place do allow a very specific cost to be quantified for one part of the operation. It is but a short step from here to the concept of a 'value-added' service, in which the information intermediary passes on to the consumer the costs incurred in obtaining the information from the supplier. What was once a purely service relationship has become a relationship between buyer and seller.

It is not only, however, in obviously value-added transactions that technology has changed the relationship between the provider and the recipient of information. The information chain itself has been radically changed, and new participants have taken the place of traditional players.

In particular, the intermediary roles are different. In the familiar chain of communication from author to reader, only the roles of these two, at either end of the chain, remain substantially unmodified, and even their perceptions of each other and of their relationship have begun to change. In the traditional model, as we have seen, the author completes the work, and hands it over to those who will take technical, financial and commercial responsibility for its production, distribution and sale. The ultimate beneficiaries, the readers, are passive recipients at the end of this process, able to obtain only what those who stand between them and the author want them to have. Technology has wrought a fundamental change in this model. Not only is it the case that the information recipient need no longer be the passive and unresponsive recipient, but also that the intermediary role of the publisher is increasingly under challenge and threat, as we shall see.

But perhaps the greatest transformation has been in personal rather than public communication, and arguably in the blurring of the boundaries between the two. E-mail, once the esoteric domain of the academic community, is now the most common form of non-voice communication throughout the world for both personal and business transactions. The providers of traditional PTT services, and especially of postal services, have seen their market undermined almost to the point of collapse. The impact has been massive. Patterns of work have fundamentally changed. In most organizations, the internal memorandum, once one of the great operational tools (and a great generator of waste paper and unnecessary files) has all but vanished, often by employee choice as much as by management decree. There is also a downside. E-mail is often treated as if it were a private conversation, which can all too easily not be the case. Sometimes an exchange of e-mails is a far less efficient way of transacting an item of business than a simple phone call, or even a walk across the room to a colleague's desk. But in broad terms, the universal adoption of e-mail has been an immense benefit. In the former communist countries of eastern Europe, for example, and in the rapidly industrializing economies of southeast Asia, the 1990s saw a leap from old-fashioned, heavily controlled and very inefficient communications processes into electronic communications on a vast scale; while international communications, especially those between time zones, have become greatly easier. All of this has been generally beneficial to the economy, if not always to the lives of those directly engaged with it, who often find themselves committed to long and ill defined working hours, and a continual stream of apparently urgent communications.

The use of e-mail has profoundly changed how people communicate with each other, but it is not the only transformative factor. Ever since the internet was first established within the scientific world where it began, it has been used by groups sharing a common interest for informal, and increasingly for formal, communications within the group. Discussion groups began in the 1980s, at first bringing together scattered communities of specialists who could rarely meet. Such groups have proliferated, and, as the use of the internet spread outside the academic sector in the 1990s, they began to cater for every imaginable variety of social interest. The commercial ISPs began to provide tools to allow groups to be established and to operate; they now host thousands of groups, whose membership varies from a handful to hundreds of thousands, and perhaps in some cases millions. There are few if any activities and interests which are not the focus of at least one virtual group of this kind. Discussion groups are, in a sense, the electronic equivalent of an open meeting. In effect, tens of thousands of virtual communities of interest have been created, through which people from all over the world can pursue their common concerns.

The early discussion groups focused on shared professional concerns. Among their common uses were (and are) advertising job vacancies, and calls for research proposals in the academic world, as a substitute for, or supplement to, traditional print-on-paper systems of information. They can be used to gather information; a subscriber can ask for help or advice, such as a bibliographic reference, an elusive fact, or the address or telephone number of someone known to the enquirer only by name. This function goes significantly beyond any conventional paper-based system; it is interactive, exploiting the communications network by allowing recipients to reply. The most sophisticated use is conducting a discussion of some issue of common interest. A subscriber poses a question to other members of the group, proposes a theory, expounds an idea or simply conveys a fact or offers an opinion. Other members of the group can react and respond, while some may choose to be passive observers of a particular interchange. This is quite different from the simple model of a mailing system, or even an interactive information and enquiry service. Used in this way, a discussion group is a forum for semi-public discourse. Perhaps the nearest traditional analogy is that of the correspondence columns of a newspaper, but the comparison is not particularly helpful. No one has the authority to stop or interfere with a particular interchange, and everyone has the right to intervene in it, although in practice some lists are more formally moderated, and all the service providers have basic rules about harmful or offensive material.

Even less formal versions of the discussion group emerged on the web in the late 1990s; these included the 'guest book' and the 'chat room'. Visitors to a website will find a guest book in which they can record, by e-mail, their opinions, ask a question, or simply seek to make contact with other visitors. Guest books are maintained by the site's owner, who can impose rules, and can remove unacceptable postings. Chat rooms are exactly what the name suggests. A visitor can enter a website's chat room to discuss matters of common interest with other visitors. On some sites there is a degree of mediation, or at least a set of rules and protocols, but on others there is little or none. The chat room is essentially a creature of the internet, as near as we have yet come to electronic discussion in a mode close to casual conversations. Unlike the mediated discussion groups, guest books and chat rooms are probably most used for social and recreational purposes; they have opened up powerful new mechanisms through which individuals anywhere in the world who share a common interest can 'meet' each other. This is a wholly new medium of communication. They can also pose great dangers. One of the most common uses of chat rooms is to 'meet' people; meetings which move from cyberspace to reality have sometimes proved to be catastrophic.

The world wide web

Almost all of the systems and activities described in the last section have been made possible, or made easier, by the world wide web. The story of the origin of the web is remarkable in itself. Like the internet, it has its origin in the scientific research community, in this case at CERN, the European nuclear research facility in Geneva, Switzerland. Tim Berners-Lee, an English physicist employed as an information and computing specialist, was seeking a way of capturing the vast amounts of knowledge and information held in the organization, and in particular that which was accumulated comparatively informally by the scores of visiting scientists who came to work at CERN. He found the solution in the concept of hypertext, first proposed by an American computer scientist, Ted Nelson, in the mid-1960s. By 1991, Berners-Lee had a working system; four years later, the web accounted for 25% of all internet traffic, and then the real explosion began.

The essence of hypertext (which is more properly now called hypermedia, since it incorporates audio and video as well as text) is that it facilitates rapid and direct movement from one part of a file to another, and between files. The creator of a website builds in links to other pages which, by a click on the mouse, allow the user to move to that page. This may be a page on the same site or it may be elsewhere; the possibilities are limitless, and indeed the location of the information is of no concern to the end-user. Sites themselves have internet addresses, derived from the system used for e-mail addresses. Websites are identified by Uniform Resource Locators (URLs), which provide a global access system, analogous to internationally recognized telephone numbers. The system of URLs was developed at the same time as the web itself, largely by the American Jon Postel, whose organization, the Internet Assigned Numbers Authority (IANA), controlled the issue of URLs, as its successor still does. The form of the URL, combining the organization's name, its domain (such as .edu, .com, .gov, and so on) and (usually, except in the USA) a country name (.uk, .de), has become a part of daily life for millions of people throughout the world.

It is now normal practice for almost all organizations to have their own websites. They have become an integral part of the information and marketing strategy of everything from airlines to zoos. Simultaneously, a whole new web-based culture has developed. Individuals can establish their own sites (or home pages) and use them to provide whatever information or opinion they choose. All that is needed is access to a host computer (the server) linked to the internet, and the very basic technical skills needed to use an appropriate mark-up language (usually XML or HTML) – the programming code in which web data are written – or, even more easily, a web editor. Browsing this global databank has become, for some people, a hobby that verges on an obsession; from its earliest years it attracted the metaphor of the classic Californian activity of surfing.

The web, however, is more than merely an advertising tool or a toy. It has vast implications for the future of information service provision and the communication of information. In effect, the 'owner' of the site is a publisher, but a publisher upon whom there are no significant external controls. The quality control – even at the level of basic factual accuracy – that traditionally typifies all but the most ephemeral and peripheral publishing is completely missing from the web. All that exists is a voluntary constraint imposed by webmasters on themselves, or by site owners, and perhaps by the ISPs, on their webmasters. Individuals can – and do – publish whatever they want. Whether this is electronic democracy at work, or merely a worthless electronic anarchy, it has certainly become in part the electronic equivalent of vanity publishing – but without incurring any significant direct costs and with an automatic global distribution system.

The exponential growth of the web and indeed of the internet as a whole has created its own problems. The information superhighway (a favourite metaphor of progressive politicians in the early 1990s) is all too often like an overcrowded and undersized city street in the rush hour, with traffic barely moving and offering little more than frustration and mounting costs for travellers. For all its universality, the internet is fragile and vulnerable. The demand for network usage is growing more quickly than the physical infrastructure which sustains it, and response times from URLs are often unacceptably slow, especially outside the comparatively protected sphere of the academic networks. Moreover, the system, like a grid system which supplies electric power, can be exposed to domino-like failures. In the summer of 1997, two interlinked computer crashes in Virginia brought a large part of the internet to a halt for nearly 24 hours, with repercussions across the globe. In 1999, the Melissa virus, developed by an American computer nerd with a grievance against the world at large, came frighteningly close to destroying the whole system. The reliability of both the information itself and the information system cannot be guaranteed, and the inevitably continuing reliance on the internet will further expose its potential weaknesses. Such attacks are becoming more frequent and more damaging, as exemplified in the worldwide dissemination of the My Doom virus in 2004, conceived, it seems, as a deliberate assault on Microsoft.

Perhaps the most urgent issue that faced the web as it evolved so quickly in the mid-1990s was that of navigation. Where was the map of the information superhighway? The answer lay in the development of search engines, which would respond to a user's query by searching the web for appropriate pages. All web users are now familiar with how these systems work, at least superficially, to the extent that globally available engines such as Yahoo! and Google have became major businesses in their own right, and as dominant in their sphere as one or two major systems providers are in theirs. The efficacy of a search engine, however, depends on its capacity to search quickly for the information the user is seeking, and that in turn is dependent on the information (metadata) provided by the content creator and the website owner. Simple searches are not generally a problem, but more complex searching is potentially a highly skilled task. Since the vast majority of users neither have nor wish to acquire these skills, the burden falls on the providers of content and search engines, who need the skills of information professionals to ensure that metadata is provided and made accessible to facilitate complex and efficient searching. Although this is happening to some extent, even the more complex manifestations of the major search engines can still produce millions of 'hits' if the search is not carefully framed. This has significant implications for the education of future as well as current generations. It is not merely ICT skills that will be essential; indeed technical expertise will become less important as technology becomes even more robust and user-friendly. But information skills will be fundamental, and urgently need to be incorporated in education programmes from the earliest years of a child's life.

The evolution of the web to the point at which it is, at least in common parlance, virtually synonymous with the internet itself, was a key development of the last few years of the 20th century. The discussion groups and other facilities discussed in the previous section of this chapter continue to exist and indeed to flourish, but since the turn of the millennium this has been further developed as the platform for a whole new approach to networked communications. What is sometimes called the 'social web' or 'Web 2.0' uses the technological platform of the internet and the familiar interfaces and structures of the web to link people rather than documents. Sites such as Facebook provide a mechanism for individuals to project their own personalities (real or invented) and to meet people with shared interests and concerns. Making 'friends' online has become fashionable, and is having a significant impact on how individuals interact with each other. Critics say that the social sites encourage unhealthy fantasies; others see it as a harmless expression of youthful high spirits. It can certainly be argued that the social web, ironically, leads to social isolation in the real world. Teenagers sit alone at their laptops rather than going out to meet real people in real situations. The longer-term consequences cannot yet be predicted.

Social sites are not the only manifestation of the latest phase of the evolution of the web. Blogs and wikis are perhaps even more familiar, and possibly even more widely used. Like so many of the facilities which the internet can offer, blogs ('Weblogs') can be used for a multitude of purposes. At one end of the spectrum is the individual who regularly posts egotistical reflections on his or her life and opinions, and at the other is the journalist in a country with heavy press censorship using blogs as a means of telling the world what is really happening. The latter phenomenon has been found in recent years in Iraq, Zimbabwe, China and other countries where freedom of expression is limited or dangerous. A wiki (the term derives from a word meaning 'easy' in the Hawaiian language) was in origin a piece of software which allowed collaborative creation of a web page by groups of people with minimal technical skills. Its key characteristic is that it was collaborative in nature. The Wikipedia, which is perhaps the most familiar product of wiki software, is a perfect example; anyone can contribute (although there is some editorial intervention) which means that it is completely open, but also that it is not wholly reliable. Like many of the other developments in the communication of information in the last twenty years, the wiki has put much of the onus for the verification of information on the end-user rather than the information provider.

Networks: an electronic democracy?

The systems that have been briefly described in the last two sections of this chapter are now familiar to tens of millions of people throughout the world, young and old alike. Indeed, there are few significant organizations in the world which do not have a website; almost all sites have some mechanism for electronic feedback and discussion, which may vary from a click-on e-mail address to a sophisticated and secure system for ordering goods or services. For some users all of this is 'free'. In most countries, governments, research organizations and the universities (or their funding agencies) support the computing and communications networks which facilitate the operation of the system without direct charge to end-users. These networks are complex and expensive. They are dependent on a sophisticated infrastructure which includes computers with massive processing and storage capacity, usually at each major site of usage (each university, for example), as well as effective telecommunications systems (sometimes along specially dedicated lines) to link them. Each server is linked locally to workstations from which individual users access the system. The infrastructure itself has to be installed, maintained and regularly enhanced as usage increases and the technology is constantly changed and improved. The origin of the networks was almost casual, but it has now been formalized. In Britain, SuperJANET links the universities and other academic bodies, and is widely available to other subscribers. International links between national and regional systems created the internet itself, originally sponsored by the National Science Foundation in the USA. The internet had revolutionized communications in the academic and research communities in the developed world by about 1990, but its breakthrough into the wider world, and particularly into the home, was a development of the mid-1990s associated with the world wide web. The exponential growth of network access inevitably meant that there was a move towards commercial provision of services.

The private sector was initially somewhat less enthusiastic about e-mail and its associated facilities than academics and others in public sector environments. The emergence and mushroom growth of private-sector internet service providers (ISPs) was another aspect of the cyber-revolution of the late 1990s. From 1995 onwards, the Microsoft Network (MSN) was an integral part of the Windows operating system which dominated the personal computer market around the world. Competitors included such companies as Freeserve (in the UK) and America On-Line (AOL) (in the USA and everywhere else). By the mid-1990s, the normal practice was for service provision to be free, with the user incurring only telecommunications charges, and the provider being supported by advertising. The software itself was typically distributed on free CD-ROMs which came with magazines, newspapers, advertising materials or simply as mailshots. MSN itself is an integral part of the operating system and software package which is provided with virtually every PC in the world. Some of the ISPs were in the forefront of the 'dotcom' bubble, achieving paper values which did not always reflect their profitability or their prospects. But the commercial power of the ISPs is very real, exemplified by the takeover by AOL of Time-Warner, a global communications company which, as we saw in Chapter 3, had already absorbed venerable publishing houses and one of the great Hollywood studios of the golden age of the cinema.

Quite apart from being the subjects of commerce in their own right, the ISPs have transformed the way in which business is done. E-mail permits easy communications between time zones. To make a telephone call from London to Los Angeles during ordinary business hours in both cities is almost impossible; at 5.00 pm in London, it is 9.00 am in Los Angeles. When there are also the complications of different working weeks (in Islamic countries, for example, where the weekend is normally Thursday and Friday or Friday and Saturday), the problem is even more acute. E-mail overcomes this; the message is sent during normal hours, and is read when the recipient next accesses the system. The reply can then be generated and sent; it will be waiting when the original sender next logs on. Thus, for example, a message can be sent from London at noon on Monday, and can be read in Sydney at 9.00 am on Tuesday (eleven hours later); an immediate reply can be read in London at 9.00 am on Wednesday. In the interchange, no one has had to make or take telephone calls at hours of the night when they might not be functioning at their best; on the other hand, airmail would be slower (by several days) and fax would be less secure, since an e-mail message can only go directly from sender to recipient because of the password protection of the file stores in each person's computer. Such advantages have commended themselves to many businesses, and the use of e-mail and its associated facilities can be expected to continue to grow.

The internet is also supplanting some other traditional means of communications. At a time when the costs of travel and accommodation are, in real terms, increasing more quickly than the costs of communications, and travel security is seen as a real issue, electronic substitutes for meetings and conferences are inevitably attractive. Some academic conferences make use of these facilities, so that, for example, those who are unable to attend the conference can read a pre-circulated paper on a discussion list, and join in the discussion by the same means or by registering for a specially established group name for a particular conference. This may not be as satisfactory, in some ways, as being present at a meeting, but it is better than not being able to participate at all. Similar uses in the public service and in business are increasingly common.

This, however, is only the beginning of the story. The business equivalents of chat rooms are password-protected areas of cyberspace in which global business meetings can take place without incurring travel costs or paying hotel bills. Again, it was the academics who pioneered this, using discussion groups as quasi-conferences in which papers (sometimes in advanced draft rather than a final version) could be posted for comment by other people in the subject community. In the business sector, of course, security and confidentiality are of great significance, and passwords and even the encryption of data do not provide complete protection. Nevertheless, for many purposes electronic discussion is acceptable, and is radically changing the economics of business and the social structure of businesses themselves and of the domestic arrangements of participants.

The use of the internet to facilitate the conduct of business within an organization, or between organizations, is only one dimension of the changes wrought in the commercial world. At the present time, it is the development of e-commerce which dominates public perceptions of the commercial use of the internet. In a slightly different context, we have already touched on the impact of e-commerce on the bookselling trade; but it is not only books that are sold online. Everything from groceries to machine guns can be bought through websites.

All of this, however, is ultimately dependent on the availability of reliable and accessible networks. The need for greater bandwidth, which facilitates not only quicker transmission of data but also the transmission of the much larger data packages necessary for audio and video as opposed to textual matter, was a real problem by the turn of the millennium. The gradual expansion of broadband networks, both wired and wireless, has provided the infrastructure through which content can be delivered. This has been a very significant commercial development for the telecommunications industries, but it has also brought about new areas of competition and convergence in the information industry itself. The initial penetration of broadband into the domestic market was typically through the telecommunications companies, but satellite television providers also saw a means of exploiting their technologies to compete in this market. In many western counties this competition is now both direct and intensive. On the one hand telecoms providers offer an increasing range of content as well as voice and data communications, while satellite broadcasting networks are beginning to provide facilities for voice and data communications as well as access to broadcast content. In neither case is the combination yet wholly satisfactory, but it seems likely that commercial imperatives will drive further technical developments to make the systems more acceptable to the end-user.

Already, however, the networks are being used for an ever increasing range of applications, some with consequences far beyond what was initially imagined, perhaps even by their creators. The music industry is being shaken to its foundations by the consumer-driven shift from sales on portable media (such as CDs) to sales by download directly to the consumer's own storage medium. Some artists are beginning to put their own pressure on the music companies to move to this means of sales and distribution, which they believe to be more popular and hence more profitable. Even in the much smaller and possibly more conservative business of classical music, downloads are making inroads into the market. The proliferation of storage and listening devices, exemplified by the increasingly ubiquitous iPod, both reflects this trend and accelerates it.

The rapid development of information and communication systems and devices in the last decade has changed professional, social, commercial and political relationships. It has opened up new channels of communication in which individuals and groups can propagate their views almost without any limitations. We are still in the midst of these changes, and it is perhaps not possible to predict where (if at all) change will end; and at least some of its consequences are not yet fully understood. We can however perhaps see two major trends. On the one hand, informal patterns of information flow are becoming more open and more accessible. On the other hand, more formal communications systems are also being transformed by making use of the same technologies but in a different way. This point can be exemplified by considering recent developments in the publication of scientific and other scholarly journals.

Electronic publishing: towards a new paradigm?

The basic principle of the electronic journal is derived from the traditional model of the scholarly or scientific periodical. Such periodicals all operate in a similar way, although there are differences between disciplines. Contributors submit papers for publication, usually based on recent research or perhaps on a review of previous work in the field; the editor reads the submissions, or (more often) sends each to one or more specialist advisers ('referees') who will assess its suitability for publication. The paper may then be rejected, accepted as it stands, or (very commonly) returned to the contributor for revisions in the light of the referees' comments. In due course, it is accepted in its final version and printed in the next available issue of the journal. The whole process may take between three and twelve months depending on the subject matter, the importance of the paper and the traditions of different academic disciplines, as well as less predictable factors such as the efficiency of the editor and the willingness of potential referees to undertake the work. This is the classic model of scholarly communication; it has served the academic world well for over a century.

The earliest experiments with electronic journals (or online journals as they were often, and significantly, called) tried to convert this model into an electronic format. Contributors submitted their papers electronically to a computer which could be accessed by the editor. The editor read the paper in this form, and perhaps sent it to a referee's computer; the referee's comments were returned electronically to the editor, who transmitted them, perhaps suitably modified and certainly anonymized (as is the custom with referees' reports) to the authors. In other words, the traditional process was simply replicated in electronic form, including an electronic version of the quality control which is the reason for the editing and refereeing process.

All of this was comparatively easy, and became easier with the growth of the public access networks. Contributors, editors and referees communicate using the internet, to which, almost without exception, they will have unlimited access. Most potential readers are in the same position. It is, however, precisely at this final and crucial stage, when the work is to be transmitted to the reader, that the real difficulties begin. Although this may seem to be simply the electronic equivalent of publication, no simple substitution of electronic for paper-based methods is possible. To understand the problem it is necessary to consider the business model that underpins how scholarly and scientific journals are traditionally published and distributed.

Learned journals are owned by publishers, which comprise either publishing houses or learned societies, or sometimes the two working together. Editors and referees (and occasionally contributors) may receive small fees for their work, although this is not a major factor either for the publishers or for the editors and referees: the fees are small because the real rewards lie in the academic recognition (which may generate financial rewards in other ways, such as by promotion) rather than money. The real costs to the publisher lie in printing and distribution. Typically, the journal is published between four and six times a year, and the annual issues are cumulated into a volume, usually with an index. Print runs are often small (as low as 250 in some cases), but distribution is worldwide. On the other hand, money for subscriptions (almost all of it from libraries) is collected annually in advance to provide working capital; distribution is undertaken by agents who make their own profits by charging a premium for the services which they provide. The economics of journal publishing are by no means impossible, but journals have nevertheless, and with some justification, become very expensive, with subscriptions of several hundred pounds being by no means uncommon, and those of many thousands not unknown. As a result, in times of economic constraint, many libraries have been forced to cancel subscriptions, thus further decreasing the print runs and increasing the prices.

Conceptually, it was not difficult to design a system which could replace printed publication by electronic distribution, and even to devise mechanisms of charging and payment to support the operation. In practice, however, there is a major obstacle. The scholarly communication system which has developed around the refereed journal has come to occupy a place of central importance in the academic world. Individual academics, and their departments and universities, are judged for many purposes by the quality and even the quantity of their published output. When that output is in the pages of a journal which is known to be strictly controlled to the highest standards by editors and referees, it is particularly prestigious and can have a major influence on individual and institutional success.

The system depends largely on peer-group acceptance of it, although there are some allegedly more objective measures which can be used. The most important of these are derived from citation indexes which show the number of citations of a particular paper in other publications. In practice, however, it is publication in the 'right' journals which really matters, and several investigations in the 1980s and 1990s suggested that scientists and others were reluctant to accept electronic journals as being the equivalent, in qualitative terms, of traditional print-on-paper learned journals. This seems to have been partly because of suspicions about the robustness of the refereeing, partly because of concerns about the permanence of the journal itself, and partly because of the fear that electronically published papers would not be so widely accessible and hence not be so often cited as papers published in the traditional format. As a result, early electronic journals did not attract high-quality papers, and consequently they continue to fail to attract the very papers which alone could improve their prestige. This vicious circle was partly caused by the general reluctance to change – which is no less common among the most innovative of intellectuals than it is elsewhere in society – but some causes were more rational; they were related to the distribution and access mechanisms of the electronic journal. In practice, most electronic journals were merely a web-delivered version of a printed journal which is still published in conventional format. This is easily identifiable from the visual appearance. Almost all electronic journals use the PDF format which gives the appearance of a printed page. This was not merely the product of academic conservatism; it was because the electronic publication is a spin-off from the printed version. The initial reluctance has now been overcome, and after the turn of the millennium electronic publication of journals developed very quickly in all disciplines, but it continues to be unusual for a journal to be published only in an electronic format.

The creation of parallel electronic and print products is a direct consequence of the traditional business model for journals. The essence of it is the fact that journals are bought by libraries on subscription, and are thus available to all the users of a particular library. Moreover, individual papers are accessible to the users of non-subscribing libraries through interlibrary lending or document delivery systems, which usually involve the provision, for private use, of a photocopy or PDF file of a particular paper. The economics of journal publication leaves little margin for error, but the system does work, and it is possible to publish scientific and learned journals at a price which the market will tolerate. The calculations do not, however, easily accommodate radical change, especially of the size and scale implicit in switching from paper-based to electronic publication and dissemination.

A traditional journal is paid for by a library in much the same way as it buys a book; it is true that the payment is a subscription, but the basic principle – buying an information carrier which becomes a common-user tool – is the same. Only in a very limited way can anything like this apply to an electronic journal. One model for such a journal is that 'subscribers' buy access to the database in which the papers are held, and, as in accessing any other database, pay for both the telecommunications charge and for access to the information itself. Such charges might be paid by an individual or by an institution, but even in this simple model there has already been a critical shift of emphasis. The traditional journal is bought by a library for general access; individual usages of it are neither quantified nor costed in normal circumstances, as we have already seen in the slightly different, but fundamentally similar, case of public library usage. Access to an electronic journal, however, can be very precisely costed, and identified with a particular library user. Who will pay the charges that are incurred? Whatever the answer (which is determined by a combination of political and economic factors) we no longer have here a model of common access to a common resource. In practice, library subscriptions to journals now include both the printed and the electronic versions. Users can choose which version they use. Libraries typically buy a 'bundle' of subscriptions from a publisher or agent; this is a predefined package of subscriptions to which the individual library can add more titles at extra cost. For the end-user there is the convenience of electronic access, including simultaneous access by more than one user. For the librarian, the medium-term advantage is that they need not store the printed version (although many choose to do so) since any future user can access the electronic archive. There are some genuinely electronic journals, i.e. journals of which there is no printed version. But they have been slow to develop, partly because of the economic model on which they are based, which is quite different from that of a traditional printed journal. There are, of course, some parallels. The database, in this model, is owned by a publisher, just as a publisher owns the title and often the copyright in the papers of the traditional journal. The publisher of the database, like the traditional journal publisher, takes financial risks in order to produce the journal. These risks are high, but the income is no longer either so predictable or so conveniently collected. Under the traditional system, the annual advance subscription means that the print run need not exceed the demand. Indeed, it is normally tailored to it almost exactly, so that there are few spare copies, and individual issues of the journal go 'out of print' almost as soon as they are published. The money to support this operation is received in advance of costs being incurred; typically, subscriptions fall due on 1 January, and a quarterly is normally published in March, June, September and December. Printing and distribution costs for the year are not even incurred until the bulk of the subscription income has been received, and some of it can be held back (earning interest) for as long as 12 months.

No such certainty is possible for the publisher of an electronic journal offering instantaneous access to a continuously augmented database. First, the publisher must buy (or rent) sufficient computer storage space not merely for the current issue, but for all previous issues of the journal. This is essential if the electronic journal is to compete with the prestige of the printed journal which, despite going out of print almost immediately after it is published, is nevertheless available in libraries or through document delivery services in perpetuity. With an electronic journal, this permanent availability can be achieved only by permanent electronic storage. Electronic archiving has become a major issue in the academic community and among librarians and publishers. The advocates and producers of electronic journals are still confronted by a real problem: the use of an essentially ephemeral communications technology for the permanent storage of data which may be intermittently and unpredictably required over long periods of time.

The model of electronic archiving which is now beginning to predominate has a central file store from which the papers for many different journals can be retrieved, offering an electronic surrogate for a document delivery system rather than for a single journal. Again, there are economic issues to be resolved, but moving closer to the model of a library rather than a publisher at least opens up the possibility of public sector involvement. Electronic journal archives – some subject-based and some more general – are now provided by a number of public agencies and commercial publishers. At the same time, universities and research institutes are developing their own digital repositories in which their staff are asked (and sometimes required) to deposit their published work. Subject to considerations of copyright, these repositories can be open to everyone. The combination of subject-based and institutional repositories will probably be the way of the future. It is at least possible that commercial publishers will find themselves squeezed out of the process as learned societies and universities themselves play a more active role in the storage and dissemination of the research outputs that their staff produce.

All the systems and products discussed in this and the previous three sections of this chapter illustrate both the potential and the limitations of the use of information technology. All of them offer great advantages over the traditional methods of information storage and transfer which they have replaced, or indeed offer facilities which no traditional system could have provided. The most important difference is probably that of immediacy. Electronic communications are, for all practical purposes, instantaneous;

the delays caused by 'traffic jams' in the network, or temporary overload on individual computers, are comparatively trivial compared with the delay in publishing and distributing traditional newsletters, printed journals and books. Moreover, all of these systems, to a greater or lesser extent, allow some form of participation in an active partnership rather than the mere passive reception of information. At one end of the scale, e-mail and electronic discussions are, by definition, interactive, but even the formal electronic journal is as accessible as its printed equivalents within its own communities. The internet makes all public information in the system widely available. By exploiting search engines, which permit unlimited and uncharged access and searching on a global basis, it is possible to find discussion lists, and the 'archived' products of public electronic discourse, using any computer with network access.

The development of the global web-based network (which took less than five years) was perhaps the greatest revolution in communications since the 15th century, but no revolution is without its disadvantages. There are some less favourable factors to be considered. The use of all the systems which have been described depends on access to a network which links the individual user to the computer in which the information which is being sought is stored, or which facilitates the communication which is being attempted. At one level this is familiar. We expect to need, and to pay for, a telephone before being able to make telephone calls. We expect to pay the cost of postage when sending a letter. Indeed, we expect to pay an appropriate price when we buy a book or subscribe to a journal or newsletter, but we have also developed systems which allow books and journals to be bought at general expense using public funds, in return for general access in libraries. It is this transaction, and the social and cultural assumptions and expectations which underpin it, which is being challenged by the electronic systems we have discussed in this chapter.

The true cost of network access is high; this is not altered by the fact that, for many users, it is hidden and may indeed generate savings elsewhere in such diverse areas as secretarial services and library provision. Some technical skills are needed in order to gain access, although they are basic and simple. More importantly, however, the potential user needs some understanding of the operation of the network and of the structure of the information itself in order to use it effectively. Although the knowledge base and skill level are of no higher order than those needed to use a book, they are not always instinctive even in users of high intelligence who are familiar with other information media. Just as we have to be taught to read and write, and how to use a table of contents or an index, we have to be taught how to search a database, use a search engine, or send and manipulate e-mail These are indeed skills which, once acquired, seem so basic as barely to be skills at all, but, like all skills, they have the effect of excluding those who do not possess them. Moreover there is no evidence to suggest that we have a reached a point of stasis in the development of information systems and services; indeed, the evidence is strongly to the contrary. New systems and devices can be outmoded as quickly as they came into consciousness. Some simple examples include the floppy disk, now all but abandoned and largely forgotten; and the gradual, but increasingly rapid, abandonment of the audio CD as a medium for recorded music. Even e-mail, which has probably been the single most transformative factor in the whole information society revolution as far as the vast majority of people are concerned, is being seriously challenged. Messaging systems which include text, audio and video sent across wireless networks also used for speech communications are being used where e-mail would have been used only two or three years ago. The development of the social web tends in the same direction of making yet further changes in the continuously evolving systems that we use to talk to each other. Even the most experienced and skilled users – and perhaps especially they – are continually having to learn how to use new systems and new devices.

The cost of access: issues and problems

Both network access and skill development can present obstacles to the use of new electronic information and communications systems. The most important obstacle, however, remains the cost. As has been suggested throughout this chapter, there is a fundamental difference between buying a book and buying information from a database. The latter is acquired once and may be restricted to a single use or user; the former, once acquired, can be used – for all practical purposes – for ever by anyone. Even if there is no charge for the information itself, which is of course the case for the vast majority of websites, telecommunications charges are incurred and there are capital costs for hardware and software. We can ascribe the cost of a particular information transaction to the person by whom, or for whom, the transaction was undertaken. Information is no longer even perceived to be 'free' in an economic sense, however 'free' access may be in the sense that there is no legal or technical obstacle to obtaining it. The partial concealment of the cost of electronic information access through publicly funded networks does not affect the central issue, and may, in any case, be assumed to be a temporary phenomenon. We are again led towards the concept of the value which is added to information by the transactions which carry it from source to user. This value can also be costed and the end-user can therefore be charged for the transaction as a whole.

The possibility of making profits from the provision of information to individuals, by charging for information itself and for the means of obtaining it, has made great changes in the way in which we think about such provision. The traditional liberal assumptions, suggested in the first part of this chapter, are no longer as applicable as once they were. The boundaries between private and public territories, and between personal and institutional domains, have shifted dramatically. In political terms, this has expressed itself in the move from the public to the private sector which has already been mentioned, but this is merely one manifestation of a change which is driven as much by technology as it is by public policy. As the private sector takes a larger role in information provision, and as it becomes easier to assess the cost of providing information services, questions can be formulated about the role of the public sector with its apparently 'free' provision of some of the same services. In British political discourse, this question is usually addressed in terms of the definition of the public library service. Although this is, in one sense, a special case, it does also have broader and more generally applicable implications. Public libraries operate under legislation which requires them to offer an adequate service, without defining what that service is. More recent British legislation, dating from 1991, specifically allows them to charge for certain services, including loan services of recorded music and videos, and interlibrary loans, as well as for value-added services, such as online searching. The 1991 Order is permissive rather than mandatory, and there are variations between library authorities in their use of it, but charges for such services are now common.

This in itself, raises some general issues. DVD hire, for example, is a lucrative business; it was developed in the private sector (originally for videos), often by small local shops, although large chains are now major players. Public libraries which appear to compete in this market could be argued to derive an unfair advantage from their publicly funded infrastructure and economies of scale. In practice, the range of DVDs available is probably different in the two outlets, and indeed a typical hire shop probably has a significantly larger number than almost any library. The point of principle, however, remains. In some ways, the issue is similar to that raised by the competition between the BBC, funded by a general levy on the viewing public, and the commercial terrestrial and satellite channels, funded from advertising and sponsorship. The question is no longer whether the public and private sectors should compete against each other, but rather whether there should be a public, or quasi-public, sector at all.

In the public library arena, this issue increasingly revolves around the definition of the so-called 'core' services, which are provided free at the point of delivery. If it is to be little more than a basic lending and reference service from the stock in any given library, this represents a significant reduction in the level of non-charged services available to many users, such as those who use small branches or mobile libraries. If all but the most basic services are moved out of the dimension of public provision, the implication is that the private sector will provide whatever the market will sustain, but only to those who can afford to buy information services at whatever price the market will bear.

Libraries throughout the world have responded to this changing environment in different ways. Some are unashamedly competing, especially in the provision of information to business, industry and local government, and are working with the private sector and with other public sector agencies (such as university libraries, for example) in partnerships which provide high-quality services to those who seek and can afford high-value information. In other sectors, information service provision has slipped away from the public libraries, and much information which central and local government is statutorily obliged to provide in the UK is channelled through other agencies, or through the environmental and planning departments of local authorities. The public libraries are thus losing their claim to a monopoly of public information provision, even at local level. In such circumstances, it is inevitable that those who cannot afford access to information through the services provided in the private sector will, eventually, have difficulty in obtaining certain kinds of information at all. This mismatch between needs, wants and provision will be investigated in Chapter 5.

The potential for conflict (as well as competition) between the public and private sectors in library and information service delivery is not, however, confined to the public library arena. The developments which we have discussed in the communications systems which link groups of scholars, both formal (such as electronic journals) and informal (such as e-mail), call into question the role of the library in the academic community. Traditionally hailed as the heart of the university, at least in academic rhetoric, the library is in danger of becoming little more than a textbook centre, bookstore and studying space. As information technology takes more information direct to academics' and students' desks through the computers that sit on them, and indeed through the mobile devices that they carry, the library becomes just another part of the network through which they meet their information needs.

All of these matters eventually coalesce into a single issue: access to information. Technology has improved the potential for access, but at the same time it has also provided the means for restricting it. The restrictions can be determined by technical skills, technological infrastructure, political decisions and financial capacity. We return to the paradox: the potential for greater access to information has been created by the very technologies which have made it possible, and perhaps even necessary, to restrict that same access.

We should not, however, be pessimistic about this. A longer historical perspective suggests that we are only at an early stage in the revolution which is creating the information society. Many of the computer applications with which much of this chapter has been concerned are little more than a decade old as practical working systems. The number of people with some sort of access to networks, and the skills to take advantage of that access, is increasing all the time. The changing balance between the public and private domains has not yet settled into equilibrium or consensus. The political debate which will eventually determine its outcome has barely begun. We can still hope that the debate will happen, and that there will be a full consideration of the implications of providing, or not providing, effective information services in every sector of society and the economy. Past experience suggests that some time will pass, even at the present rate of technological change, before that debate is fully iterated and resolved.

In the meanwhile, the issues which the debate will address are real, and have real consequences. As information access becomes both easier and more difficult, our dependence on it increases. The overt connection between the value and the cost of information, and the ability to cost service provision as well as to valorize the information itself, are disempowering those with limited economic resources just as the increased use of networks is disempowering those with limited technical resources. Simultaneously, individuals, organizations and states which possess both wealth and skill are accumulating the potential to control information for their own advantage and to deny it to others. These are the central political issues of the information society. They will be considered in Chapters 5 and 6, as we explore how individuals and governments, and the communities which individuals constitute and governments control, are being changed by the power of information.

PART 3

The political dimension

Chapter 5

Information rich and information poor

It has been argued in Chapters 3 and 4 that information technology has both facilitated and inhibited access to information. On the one hand, it has greatly increased the ease of storing, sorting and retrieving data; on the other, it has increased the cost of doing so and made that cost more easily quantifiable. By interposing a complex technology with an expensive infrastructure between information and its potential users, it has introduced a new obstacle in the chain of supply. In a later part of this chapter, we shall explore this at the level of information supply to individuals, but it is perhaps most starkly illustrated by considering these issues in the context of states, and, in particular, the nations of the Third World and eastern Europe. This exploration must, however, begin with some more general considerations, for in Chapters 3 and 4 we have assumed that information has an economic or fiscal value. The time has now come to attempt a closer definition of that concept.

The value of information

Information is a commodity which is bought and sold. However difficult it may be to define how it acquires value, the fact of the commodification of information cannot be denied. So far, however, we have largely dealt with the financial aspects of the supply of information rather than the value of the information itself. Books, journals and computer software have a price attached to them at which they are bought and sold. We can assign costs to the construction and maintenance of telecommunications networks, computer hardware, and so on. We can calculate the cost of

processing information, in terms of the time involved in obtaining, recording and retrieving it, a cost which would normally be a combination of
paying for the time of those involved and the cost of the materials, equipment and consumables they use. None of this, however, really addresses
the question of the value - if any - which can be assigned to information.

The problem lies in part in the definition of information itself.
Dictionary definitions typically suggest that it is a subset of knowledge
acquired, deliberately or accidentally, by study or experience. For some
purposes, this is adequate: information is simply a part of the total stock
of human knowledge. We can, however, take the matter a little further. It
can be argued that the transformation of information into knowledge -
the systematization of data - depends on our ability to make records,
because the process of recording implies a process of selection. The
earliest human records, briefly discussed in Chapter 1, did not represent
the total stock of knowledge of palaeolithic man or the ancient
Babylonians, but rather that part of the knowledge store that they deemed
worthy of recording or necessary to record. Information then is
inseparable from our ability to record it.

It does not follow from this, however, that information is inseparable
from the medium on which the record is made. On the contrary, one of
the characteristics of information is that it can be transferred between
media without any significant loss of content. A hand-written sentence
might subsequently be typed, word-processed, printed, photocopied and
so on, while retaining an unchanged information content. If we add this
separability from a medium to inseparability from a recording system of
some kind, we arrive at a definition of information as a subset of
knowledge which is recorded in some symbolic form.

It is in this state, when it is independent of its medium of storage,
transmission and retrieval, that we must assign a value to information, for
it is only in this state that it has a separate existence. Economists and
information scientists (principally the latter) who have addressed this
issue are generally agreed that the user rather than the producer
determines the value of information, as opposed to its cost. The supplier
- the publisher or the bookseller - fixes the cost of a book; the value of
the information that it contains is a matter for the judgement of the

purchaser or the end-user. The value of information, therefore, is an uncertain concept, which cannot easily be quantified. Its value will be perceived differently by different people and perhaps even by the same person depending on the circumstances of time, place and context.

The variability of the value of information – determined by the consumer rather than the producer – is compounded by the fact that its value can be argued to increase as it becomes more common. This apparent paradox – that information, unlike many commodities, has no scarcity value – reflects the origin of information as a subset of knowledge. What users are seeking is the subset that best meets their needs. Up to the point at which the subset is optimized, each additional piece of information increases the value of all those that have already been acquired. Even beyond that point, there may continue to be some accumulation of value, although at a lesser rate, until the point is reached at which there is so much information that it is no longer possible effectively to use it. This is the point of *information overload*, an increasingly common phenomenon in advanced information societies.

The value of information is not intrinsic to the information itself; it depends on its suitability and availability. Yet while it is impossible to assign an absolute value to any given piece of information, it is clear that for the individual user such a value can be assigned. This may be economic, but it may also be social or cultural. The issue is how much money the end-user is prepared, directly or indirectly, to pay to acquire the information: that ultimately is the measure of its value. Some information, however, may be regarded as a public good; public health information, for example, is supplied by governments and other authorities free of charge (or rather is paid for out of general taxation). Some information may be freely provided as a form of advertising; hence the airline or railway timetables that appear on websites and elsewhere to encourage potential customers to buy the services being offered. Some information may clearly be a private good to be bought and sold by individuals for their own benefit, as when marketing information is sold to the suppliers of goods and services. A particular piece of information may actually change from private to public good or vice versa according to context.

If it is accepted that information has a value, and that this is no mere abstraction, it follows that there can be circumstances in which the absence of information is disadvantageous. In such circumstances, a person or organization (or even a country or its government) is disadvantaged because of what is not known but could be known. The uninformed or under-informed person or organization then becomes a buyer in the information market-place, provided that the information is available and that they have the resources to acquire it. This does not conflict with the concept that the value of information is determined by the end-user; indeed, it tends to reinforce it, since it is the market that provides a context in which a buyer can determine what is regarded as a fair (or at least acceptable) price.

Against this background (which is no more than a summary of one of the most complex topics in information science), we can understand the concepts of information wealth and poverty, which in turn underpin one of the most important political issues of the information society: who obtains, and who is excluded from, whatever benefits it may have to offer.

Information in developing countries: an issue defined

The value of information is not intrinsic, but lies in the uses to which it can be put. From these uses, advantages can be derived that are beneficial to the 'owner' of the information and which would not have been attainable without it. If access to information is controlled, whether fiscally or politically, the potential benefits of possessing it will be lost by those to whom it is denied. These propositions underpin the concepts of 'information wealth' and 'information poverty' and their relationship to economic development.

The furtherance of economic development lies at the heart of national policy-making in every country, whether industrialized or developing. In broad terms, it suggests the implementation of a planned series of actions leading towards the creation of an infrastructure which will support, in the long term, sustained economic activity and therefore all the other activities which that allows. Such a programme has to be designed and monitored, but it must also be sufficiently flexible to allow the design to be modified in the light of continuous analysis of the monitoring. In other words, the term 'development' implies a dynamic process, a process of change that is not random but planned, and which is aimed at achieving predetermined objectives. The long-term objectives of development are, however, not only economic, for there are also social benefits, or improvements to the quality of life. The dynamic of development, therefore, is directed not simply towards economic growth - increases in GNP, per capita output, and similar measures of economic success - but also towards less measurable benefits, such as good housing, generally accessible medical services, an efficient service sector, and a vibrant and effective civil society.

The role of the state in this process can vary. In most western countries, it is now largely confined to setting broad targets, such as inflation rates, money supply, levels of unemployment and similar macroeconomic measures. In almost all developing countries, however, the planning process is embodied in a national plan, usually based on a five-year cycle. Within such a plan, the limited resources at the command of the country are directed towards strategic objectives which have been identified as national priorities. Where there is a significant private sector in the economy, it is expected that it too will follow along the broad lines suggested by the national plan, assisted and encouraged by incentives which might take the form of relief from taxation, public investment or support for training.

If it is true that the possession of information is advantageous to the possessor, and its absence is a disadvantage, then it would seem to follow that information is essential to this developmental process. This assumption needs to be examined, and, if it is valid, must lead into a consideration of how far developing countries actually have the infrastructure needed for the provision of effective information services.

The relationship between information and development appears to be close. If, for example, we look at the most successful Asian economies - Japan, Singapore and Korea - we find that they are indeed countries in which economic and scientific information are widely and easily available. In all three, information technology has been developed and exploited to a high level of sophistication. This has led not just to the more effective management of enterprises and institutions, although that has been an important factor, but also to major structural changes in economic activities.

More widespread benefits have accrued because the key role of information in the newly industrialized countries (NICs) has not been limited to the use of information technology in government and business. It has also been critical in the development of new products, in the redesign of existing products and in the creation of new systems for the manufacturing and distribution of goods. Information systems also support the vital service sectors, such as banking, insurance, transport and the media. In other words, while the availability of scientific and technological information has been the necessary foundation for the development of science-based industries, the extended use of information technology has been necessary to create the wider infrastructure within which those industries operate. The comparative success of the information-rich economies, and the relative weakness of those that are comparatively information poor, is in itself an argument for the importance of information.

In many ways, the NICs of south-east and east Asia are more comparable to the West than they are to other Asian countries. Indeed, two of them – Japan and Singapore – have, in some respects, gone further than the West in exploiting information technology in business and industry and using the facilities which it offers in daily life. Japan, in particular, has developed a vast manufacturing sector of which information technology is an integral part, both as a tool and as a product. Japanese industry makes widespread use of robotics and computer-controlled manufacturing systems (as well as conventional business systems), but the production of information technology hardware is itself a major element in the Japanese industrial economy. Singapore has developed along different lines, using the communications capacity of information technology to turn itself, despite its small size and comparative geographical isolation from other major centres of commerce and industry, into a financial centre of global importance as well as a major port. In both countries, there are, of course, many factors at work other than the use of information technology, but it is, nevertheless, instructive that their respective governments have encouraged the development of the information industry. As a result, they successfully compete even with those western countries which also have advanced information-dependent economies.

The material success of these countries extends beyond the purely economic sector. Social development, for example in housing, welfare and medical services, and education, is possible only when there is a sound economic base which can generate the revenue needed to fund these services. In both Singapore and Japan, the economic success built on the exploitation of information technology has been used to support social development, although in different ways. Singapore, a small, tightly controlled and highly centralized state, has managed to provide a high standard of living for virtually all of its citizens, although some would argue that this has been achieved at the cost of social and political diversity. It is interesting to compare Singapore with Hong Kong in this respect, despite the profound differences in their respective political situations.

Hong Kong, perhaps to an even greater extent than Singapore, became a global financial centre in the 1980s. Historically a great trading city, it has been developed as one of the world's most important banking centres, and has consequently attracted vast investments in the financial services sector. When it reverted to Chinese sovereignty in 1997, its status as a Special Economic Zone (SEZ) was designed specifically to ensure that these benefits were not lost. As in Singapore, economic development has been possible on such a scale only because of the existence of instantaneous worldwide communications systems; these can overcome the barriers of distance and time zones which divide Hong Kong from western Europe and North America where its competitors and trading partners are, for the most part, to be found. Under British rule, however, Hong Kong, unlike Singapore, did not build a new social structure on the back of its information-technology-driven economic structure. It adhered, perhaps more strictly than anywhere else in the world, to a traditional free market economy. As a result, social development was slow and patchy, and there is a sharp contrast between wealth and poverty which is certainly more apparent than in Singapore. Hong Kong is also unlike Singapore in having a substantial manufacturing sector, but, in contrast to Japan, this sector has not, in general, benefited from the information technology revolution. The ready availability of cheap labour has allowed Hong Kong's manufacturing enterprises to retain traditional practices, which are labour intensive rather than technology based.

These examples suggest that information technology applications can be very diverse, and that both the causes and the consequences of the diversity can be political as well as economic. Singapore, Japan and Hong Kong have all, in different ways, and with different results, exploited information technology in their economic development. Each of them could be argued to be an example of an 'information society'. Each of them, however, also illustrates some of the problems that such societies can generate: uniformity and suppression of dissent to achieve economic success in Singapore; rigid social conformity in Japan; exploitation of the workforce and laggardly social development in Hong Kong, even after 1997.

The perception that the economic success of these advanced Asian economies is information based is widespread, and it is a perception which is shared in the region itself. Another of the economies of east Asia exemplifies this. Korea was one of the pioneers in implementing a national plan to provide centrally resourced information services to support science-based industry. The lesson has been learned elsewhere in Asia. In Indonesia, for example, the development of information and even library services was incorporated into national planning, and received considerable support from the World Bank and the Asia Development Bank.

The mere existence of an information service sector does not, however, guarantee success. Both India and Pakistan, for example, have for many years had scientific information centres similar to that in Korea. Neither INSDOC (Indian Scientific Documentation Centre) nor PASTIC (Pakistan Scientific and Technical Information Centre) have had the effect that was intended on their respective economies, although both provide modestly useful information services and document delivery services to scientists in universities and in industry. What is lacking are the resources which only come when there is the political will to support such services. There seems to be little of that recognition of their importance which, alone, would ensure the sustenance of a political initiative. The resources themselves, moreover, can only be found when the economy is successful enough to generate them, and that, in turn, requires a strong infusion of information services, skills and technology. When the economy does begin to take off, the secondary sectors also need information for their effective evolution and operation. This is, perhaps, most obvious in the educational field, where even the most elementary level needs some information resources for teachers, even if not for the students. Indeed, it might be argued that information is at least as vital in the secondary sectors of the economy as it is in the primary wealth-producing sectors. In some countries, this is indeed recognized. Even in China, for example, with a tradition of centralization which goes back for centuries before the communist revolution of 1949, it is now acknowledged that market information which will help to sell products is at least as important as the technical information which will help to produce them.

These arguments do not only apply in the industrial and services sectors. They apply to agriculture, which is the most basic industry for many countries in Asia, Africa and Latin America. Scientific agriculture, seeking to maximize crop yields, to eliminate disease and to preserve the quality of the land for future generations, is dependent upon the knowledge of the scientists, and hence on the information sources to which they need access. Agricultural development cannot be achieved without the effective exploitation of information, although, as in other sectors, political, economic and cultural factors can intervene to prevent the effective use of information even when it is theoretically available.

The need for information as a part of the process of development seems to be well established and is coming to be well recognized. Let us turn now to the question of how that information is to be provided. Superficially, the answers are very simple. All that is needed are good accessible information resources, good communications systems and an adequate supply of trained personnel. Those simple requirements are not quite so easily realized in practice, and need to be considered in more detail. Such consideration will bring us closer to the central issue of information provision in developing countries, and hence to the relationship between information provision and social and economic development.

Wealth and poverty: information and economic development

The phrases 'information rich' and 'information poor' need to be more precisely defined if this point is to be developed. 'Information rich' is taken to mean a country, an organization or an individual with the information which is needed to carry out the task in hand. 'Information poor' can then be defined in opposite and negative terms to describe those who lack that information. We must, however, be careful not to equate information wealth and information poverty with particular kinds of information supplied through particular media or institutions. The farmer who knows the annual patterns of the weather and of the water level in the river which irrigates his land may have sufficient information to grow an adequate crop to feed his family. In that sense he is information rich. The farmer's information wealth, however, is only comparative. If he wishes to increase the yield of his land and grow cash crops, or if he wishes to change crops, or if he wishes in any way to modify the traditional patterns to which he works, then he will need to enrich his information resources. If he cannot, he becomes a victim of information poverty, and will suffer in comparison with those who do have access to information.

This homely example can usefully be pursued a little further, for it opens up a number of important themes. It can be argued that the farmer who wants to change traditional patterns of work has already obtained information beyond that which he needed in order to work in the traditional way. He knows that change is possible. He may have observed it on his neighbour's land. He may have heard about it on the radio, or seen programmes about it on television. He may have been told about it by an agricultural adviser employed by the government or by some other agency. The intermediary is irrelevant; what is important is that the farmer has acquired information. Without that, he would not have known that change was possible. Having obtained it, he can – perhaps with more help and advice – begin to evaluate it and consider whether the change is desirable or necessary. In order to make changes, he needs yet more information about how to achieve new patterns of production and work. Most obviously, he will need to know about seeds and chemicals. He may need to know about machinery and equipment. At a secondary level, however, he will also need information: about sources of supply of these items, and almost certainly about how he can obtain the money that will be necessary to provide the initial capital for his new enterprise.

This sequence of events can be considered as a possible model for the connection between information provision and the development process. Our farmer was originally self-sustaining, and needed only that information which he had obtained when he first began to work, almost certainly orally, and probably from within the family. He then became aware of the possibility of change. This awareness arose out of his access to sources of information. He then took a decision to make changes. His next step was to seek further information about how to implement this decision, and almost immediately he was seeking information about services as well as goods. To improve his economic status, he could no longer confine his activities to one sector of the economy, but had to have access to others. At each stage, information was the catalyst that first created awareness, and then facilitated decision-making and implementation.

Another way of expressing this is to say that the farmer realized that his information wealth was only superficial; when he recognized the possibility of change, he was also recognizing the need to remedy his relative information poverty. The details of this model may not be universal, and perhaps few, if any, of those who conform to it would recognize it as a description of what they are doing, but it is, nevertheless, broadly accurate and widely applicable. As more information is acquired, more becomes necessary to implement the decisions based on the analysis of newly acquired information. The process is cyclical as well as progressive. It is a model which combines all the essential features of awareness of the need for information and access to appropriate sources and systems.

Information delivery systems: some contrasts

The appropriateness of the information delivery systems is particularly important in this context. Chapter 2 looked at the development of the many ways in which information can now be delivered to end-users, and Chapters 3 and 4 considered various aspects of the delivery mechanisms.

This chapter looks at some contrasting situations.

We normally receive information by hearing it or by seeing it, but, as we have seen, these basic sensory functions can be addressed in many different ways. We may hear information on a one-to-one basis, or in a group, or in a public speech; we may hear it privately from someone in another location through a telephone or a two-way radio; we may hear it through a public medium such as broadcast radio, or pre- recorded audio tape. Some of these media may be partly visual, like the public speech. Other media are heavily dependent on visual impact, most obviously television, video and cinema, and, of course, the screen of a computer. A particular piece of information can be transmitted by any or all of these methods, although some are more effective than others in particular circumstances. The choice of medium is critical in ensuring that the message which it conveys reaches its intended recipient and can be effectively exploited when it is received.

The effectiveness of the information transfer process depends on the effectiveness of the communication system through which the transfer is to take place, and that, in turn, depends on whether the target audience has access to the medium and can understand the message it conveys. Our farmer may be illiterate, but an illiterate person can absorb information through television or some other aural or visual medium. At a macro-level, however, the very technologies that have made the information transfer process so much more effective, have, as has already been argued, emphasized and perhaps increased the differences between the information rich and the information poor.

Technology is beginning to provide some of the answers to some of the problems it has created. The advent of CD-ROM meant that online access is no longer the only way into complex databases. As we have seen, although the CD-ROM is inevitably a little less current than the database of which it is a copy, it is both easier to use and more economical to produce than its printed equivalent, and can, of course, be updated rather than merely supplemented at regular intervals. The hardware needed for access to CD-ROMs is comparatively inexpensive, and is both cheap and easy to maintain compared with the high capital and running costs of online access. CD-ROM has the effect of removing the telecommunications element from the information technology equation. This is of the utmost importance in developing countries, where the telecommunications infrastructure is often weak, and the technology for transmitting digitized data often does not exist.

There is even greater potential in mobile telephony. CD-ROM can provide access to individual databases and sets of documents. The mobile phone has the capacity to provide access to the full range of networked information and communication services. The infrastructure for mobile telephony exists in most countries, in the form of network providers and microwave transmitters. The use of mobile phones for voice communications is rapidly becoming universal as is the suite of associated text facilities. In parts of Asia, Africa and Latin America the development of cellular networks has all but bypassed the need to create and maintain expensive hard-wired systems. Most mobile phones can now be used for indirect internet access just as a fixed-line telephone can be used through a modem; linking a mobile phone with a laptop or palmtop computer gives almost complete portability. Third and later generation mobile phones have direct access to the internet, with a display on the phone's own screen. There is still room for further development and refinement, not least in display quality and speed of access, but the basic technology opens up the prospect of virtually unlimited internet access not least in places where the conventional telecommunications networks are not sufficiently robust to provide reliable connectivity. The implications for developing countries are obvious.

Even so, it is clear that the most economically successful of the developing countries have been those which have invested most heavily and most expertly in the infrastructure of information technology, and in particular in the development of effective telecommunications systems for networking. The second-line Asian economies – India, Indonesia, Thailand, Malaysia and the Philippines – are rapidly following the examples of Singapore, Korea, Hong Kong and Japan, and indeed the western countries, in seeking to develop information and telecommunications systems as a high priority. There have been some unexpected but important side-effects. India, for example, has become a major location for telephone call centres. The comparatively well developed infrastructure and developments in mobile and digital technologies, together with a large population of unemployed or underemployed young graduates, has made it possible for western companies to base their enquiry services in Bangalore or Madras rather than Birmingham or Manchester. Infrastructure costs are cheaper, and wages far lower, even for a better educated workforce. And so we have the paradox that an enquiry from a person in Britain about the time of a train from Glasgow to London, or a complaint about the service provided by a gas company, or a reservation for a hotel in Venice, is dealt with on another continent. This early 21st century phenomenon can be taken to symbolize both the global impact of the information society and the globalization of economic activity. From one perspective, jobs are being exported from the West to India; in practice, many of those jobs were difficult to fill in western countries. So the other perception is that new jobs are being created where there is a surplus of labour. There may indeed be winners and losers; but it is not always easy to see which is which.

The installation of a fully developed communications and information infrastructure will, however, take time, and the cost means that their availability will still be limited. It is not difficult to envisage a situation in which an NIC is information rich at the national level, but contains large pockets of information poverty, which might even encompass the majority of the population. In some countries in Asia and in Latin America this danger has already been realized; again India is probably an example.

An associated danger is that more traditional means of access to information will be neglected. This manifests itself in several ways, of which two are particularly important. First, as we have suggested in Chapter 3, the greater part of the world's information resources takes the form of print on paper, which is still the most common medium of information dissemination. It follows, therefore, that a well organized and properly skilled publishing industry, an efficient book trade, and well stocked and well managed libraries, remain the key elements in any nation's information infrastructure, and underpin its formal education system.

Secondly, it should be remembered that beyond the small world of the professional users of information – scientists, managers, policy-makers – the most important information and communication medium is not the computer but broadcasting, and in particular television. This is true in the industrialized world, but perhaps the phenomenon is even more obvious in the developing countries. Television overcomes problems of illiteracy, and even of imperfect knowledge of language itself, by exploiting visual images. Although primarily a medium of entertainment, it can and does inform, and, in countries where it is strictly state controlled, television can be used very effectively for that purpose. Such use can, of course, take the form of propaganda, and it is perhaps inevitable that it should do so, although one of the unexpected effects of the development of satellite television has been the much wider availability of foreign programmes. These may be no more that the other side's propaganda, but some stations are genuinely informative – the Abu Dhabi based Al-Jezeera is an obvious example – in parts of the world and in languages where information is normally the monopoly of a carefully controlled state broadcaster. There are other positive uses of broadcasting. In Pakistan, for example, television, radio and pre-recorded taped material were used very effectively for many years by the Allama Iqbal Open University, the most successful of several attempts to provide such an institution in a developing country.

Books and television continue to be effective educational and informational media, despite the growth of the world wide web and other network services and facilities. In other words, we need to maintain and to develop the infrastructure needed for both printed and the broadcast media if we are to sustain a full range of information resources for developmental activities. There is a real problem here. We must never fall into the error of assuming that information can be provided only if we have access to computer-based information systems. Nevertheless, such systems do play a key role in making information available in the industrialized countries, and the evidence that this is economically significant is overwhelming. This suggests the depressing conclusion that the gap between information wealth and information poverty is widening rather than narrowing as the information infrastructure in the industrialized countries leaps even further ahead of that elsewhere.

North and South: the world publishing industry

It is a conclusion that is supported by considering other aspects of economic development in many parts of the world. The industrialized countries themselves encountered major economic difficulties in the late 1980s and early 1990s, and this inevitably had effects on their relations with the developing countries. At the turn of the millennium, the North–South divide, between the rich industrialized North and the poor agricultural South, was probably more marked than ever. As it widens, it becomes more difficult to cross. This phenomenon is as marked in the information sector as it is in other areas of social and economic activity. The point can be illustrated by considering the publishing industry.

During two centuries of expansion outside Europe, the British carried the English language to every continent. British power and influence were so pervasive that English became the international language of commerce, diplomacy and science, and has essentially retained that position long after Britain's withdrawal from empire. As a result, international publishing is dominated by books in English, of which the majority, as we saw in Chapter 3, are now published in the USA, although the UK is the source of a sizeable minority. English therefore remains the language of business, government and education in many countries in Asia and Africa, and in some countries, such as Nigeria and India, for example, English is, in effect, the only common language in which people from different ethnic or cultural groups can communicate.

For British and American publishers this is a great boon, for it means that their markets are global. Another consequence, however, is that the book trade is weak in many of the consumer countries. Buying western books means paying western prices, and, moreover, paying those prices in hard currency. This, in itself, is a major obstacle to educational development. Libraries in many Asian and African countries, including some which are certainly not at the lowest levels of poverty such as Kenya or India, are able to spend only a fraction of what they need to maintain anything like a reasonable collection of materials. This has been, and continues to be, a serious hindrance to the development of secondary and tertiary education and of academic and industrial research.

The alternative is the development of indigenous publishing, but this too has proved difficult. With the exception of India, there is no English-speaking developing country or NIC with a sufficiently large domestic base to support a flourishing publishing industry. Where such industries have developed, it has generally been for one of two reasons. There are those countries where there is a genuine competitor to English as the common language, such as Malaysia where Bahasa publishing flourishes and successive governments have encouraged its development as a national cultural policy. There are also countries, such as Kenya, Malawi and Zambia, where state or semi-state publishing houses produce primary- and secondary-level educational textbooks in local or regional languages. In both cases, however, the linguistic base of the industry effectively bars it from seeking global markets, and is a disincentive to local authors who seek a readership beyond the boundaries of their own country. As a result, even those countries which have begun to develop publishing industries are still dependent on imports for higher-level books, and are often unable to attract even their own native authors into publishing locally in world languages.

The continued dominance of English-language publishing by the British and American publishers and distributors, able to exploit huge domestic markets and global sales organizations, exemplifies the problem of the information poor of the South. The southern countries are forced to compete in an arena dominated by northern countries whose inherent economic strength rests on an infrastructure which the South cannot replicate. The creation of new channels of information transfer through new systems of communication has merely exacerbated the situation. Inadequate telecommunications are perhaps the most important technical obstacle. Until the development of the cellular networks for mobile telephony, there was very limited online access to the internet or other online services whether for academic, industrial or commercial purposes. Even fax was difficult. The South was effectively being excluded from much of the communications revolution, and as scientists and others in the industrialized countries become more reliant on electronic communications, those in some parts of the developing world suffered accordingly.

CD-ROM and third-generation mobile telephony offered at least partial solutions to the problem of access to scientific and technical information, but these *are* only partial. They do indeed give easy and comparatively cheap access to databases, but most of those are bibliographic, and assume subsequent access to document delivery services, full-text databases, CD-ROMs or the world wide web, in order to obtain the primary information. Such services are often inadequate in less developed countries, and where they do exist they are expensive. Few developing countries have succeeded in devising infrastructures for interlibrary lending and document delivery at national level, while to use international services, even when they are accessible, again involves the expenditure of rare hard currency. Only the most favoured institutions are normally able to do this. Consequently, the potential beneficiaries of information in the universities and governments and industrial enterprises of the Third World are all too often deprived of the information that they need for their further development. The growth of electronic publishing presents its own opportunities and challenges to developing countries. Where network infrastructure exists, access to electronic documents is no more technically difficult than it is in an industrialized country. The problem of course is the cost. Aid agencies and charities working in the information field are now targeting this issue by negotiating appropriate subscription bundles with publishers at rates which reflect the economic capacity of the customer organizations, by putting aid funding directly into subscription payments and – crucially – by developing the skills of information professionals and others so that they can make best use of the facilities which are available to them.

The cycle of information poverty, and its consequences, is only too obvious when we consider the gap between the North and the South. It does seem, however, that the cycle can be broken. Malaysia and Indonesia, for example, had apparently begun to do so by exploiting their natural resources to generate the essential hard currency which allowed them to buy the tools and expertise that they needed for the next stage of development. Thailand was moving down the same road although not without much difficulty and economic pain. The potential danger to all three countries was graphically illustrated by the near-collapse of their currencies in 1997 and the subsequent economic recession, accompanied in Indonesia by serious political instability. There are signs of recovery, especially in Malaysia, but the lesson has been a salutary one. In all three cases, large and broadly homogeneous populations (although there are minorities, mainly ethnic Chinese, in all of them) were mobilized to provide the labour which can still, to some extent, compensate for the lack of technology in the early stages of development. Nothing, however, could compensate for inadequate information infrastructures, and in all three countries the development of these infrastructures is now a priority. In this way, they are breaking through into the ranks of the newly industrialized. Although it is extremely difficult to demonstrate the importance of information in this process, the Asian examples suggest that there is a link between development and the existence of an effective information infrastructure. Similar patterns can be discerned elsewhere.

Eastern Europe: a different poverty?

A very different form of information poverty existed in eastern Europe before 1989. It had been deliberately created by the totalitarian regimes which prevailed there until the end of the 1980s. Some parts of the infrastructure were well developed, but other aspects were inhibited or even forbidden. Television, for example, was a medium of propaganda and entertainment rather than of information, as radio had been before it. It was, therefore, widely available and well resourced. Telecommunications systems, on the other hand, were deliberately underdeveloped, so that there was only limited access, even for domestic phone calls. International calls, other than through intrusive operators, were normally impossible, and fax facilities were rare. Computers did, of course, exist and were widely used for scientific purposes, but again international communications were all but impossible, and so was access to international databases. This was an information poverty which was deliberately created by the state because of the dangers which it perceived in allowing its citizens easy access to information and communications systems.

Since 1989, much effort and money has been devoted to remedying these defects. New telecommunications systems, and the widespread use of information technology, are high on the list of priorities of many eastern European governments and the western countries and agencies which are supporting their efforts. It was recognized that effective communications are essential if the countries of eastern Europe are to share in the comparative prosperity of the West, even though the strain on the western economies of trying to absorb the East initially damaged the very prosperity in which the East hoped to share. In other ways, however, the eastern countries have indeed entered into the information market-place. Newspapers now compete with each other for a market share, and operate without many of the legal constraints which formerly prevented the free dissemination of information and opinion about current affairs. Satellite television is widely accessible, and with it the vast range of information and entertainment which it transmits. Book and magazine publishing has also been freed from the constraints of the censor, and books can be produced and imported without restriction. Moreover, unlike the developing countries of the South, the former socialist countries already had the basic industrial and commercial infrastructure within which a book trade and a newspaper industry can develop. Vast improvements in the telecommunications infrastructure and availability of computers have brought eastern Europe into the world of the internet and the world wide web, although in this, as in other matters, availability and affordability are very different things. Mobile telephony is becoming common. The road may be a long one, but the journey is now well advanced, symbolized by the accession of former socialist countries to the European Union in May 2004.

The limits of wealth: information poverty in the West

It is not only, however, in the developing countries or in the reviving economies of eastern Europe that information poverty is to be found. It is pervasive in the West, either by neglect or by design, although it is of a different order from the information poverty of the Third World. To understand the phenomenon, we have to make a distinction between the absence of information itself and defects in the means of access to it. The difference is fundamental, for while the former may be remediable by comparatively straightforward actions, to remedy the latter is almost always both expensive and complicated.

A simple example will illustrate the point. In Britain and the USA, ignorance of current affairs is widespread. Public opinion polls reveal that even such basic facts as the name of the prime minister or the president are unknown to a significant percentage of the adult population. Slightly more complex enquiries, such as asking respondents to identify the photographs of allegedly well known public figures, usually yield failure rates in excess of 50%. Celebrities from the worlds of pop music, the media and sport are, on the whole, more generally recognized than political leaders. Ignorance of public affairs is not a consequence of lack of opportunity, but of lack of interest. In both the UK and the USA, virtually 100% of the population have access to television, and watch it regularly; radio is universal. The names of both countries' national leaders are heard every day on both media, and their faces seen as often on television. Ignorance is deliberate, the result of exercising a choice not to know. The means of remedying the ignorance are, however, at hand; the problem is lack of interest, not lack of access to information.

Where there is defective access, or indeed no access at all, it is altogether more serious. It can exist at many levels. A household does not have access to satellite television channels unless it has the equipment on which it can receive and decode the signal. This may be a matter of choice – a conscious decision not to buy the equipment – or it may be a decision forced on the household by economic circumstances. The example is deliberately chosen as a comparatively trivial one, but the model which it suggests can be applied in more serious cases. The company without access to market information which is known to a competitor is at a disadvantage which may be insuperable. There is evidence that in all western countries women and less well educated men, and members of ethnic minorities, the elderly and poor of both sexes are under-represented among users of computers in general and the internet in particular. The scientist without network access is excluded from discussion lists, access to the web, and so on. The examples can be multiplied.

More insidious is the deliberate deprivation of information by those who seek to use ignorance as an instrument to achieve their own ends. The example of the controlled media of eastern Europe before 1989 illustrates this. The state effectively prevented information from being circulated unless it was to its own advantage; at other times it circulated misleading or false information, again for its own ends. The use of misinformation and disinformation is considered in more detail in Chapter 6; here, we need only notice its existence. Inhibition of information transfer is not, however, practised only by the state. An advertiser is deliberately selective in the information given to a potential customer; without deviating from the truth in what is said, much can be left unsaid. This is a fundamental technique for salespeople and politicians alike. When one party to a transaction is deprived of information known to the other party, the less well informed is inevitably the weaker partner. This is not only true in commercial transactions. The social security claimant who knows less about the system than the employee of the benefit agency is disadvantaged in making a case for support. Both as consumers and citizens, everyone needs information if they are to be on even approximately equal terms with the organizations with which they have to deal.

Once again, we confront the paradox of information technology. On the one hand, the dissemination of information is far easier, and far more pervasive, than ever before. On the other, the difficulty of accessing the information which can, theoretically, be so widely disseminated, has created information-rich elites, and, conversely, pockets of information poverty. Some of these pockets, as we have seen, contain whole nations and even whole regions of the world. Others are smaller, but membership of them is no less disadvantageous. In the West, the information poor are, in general, those who are also deprived in other ways. Indeed, it is impossible to avoid the conclusion that there is a link between lack of information and lack of other forms of social and economic benefit.

Information systems have, generally, been constructed by those who are literate, articulate and well educated. Even using a teletext service requires some basic information retrieval skills such as an understanding of indexing, and some elementary skills in the interpretation of instructions and the use of equipment. To use a library or to surf the web requires basic training by demonstration or reading. Making effective use of a search engine can be a skilled task, perhaps even needing the intervention of a trained information worker or someone who, although not an information worker, has acquired higher level searching skills. As the search becomes more complex or more specialized, the need for training or for access to an intermediary becomes more marked. An inability to understand the potential of the system, or to communicate effectively with those who do, can create information poverty where none should exist. The systems themselves thus place an additional barrier between the information and its potential beneficiary.

The information poor in industrialized countries are generally being deprived of information which is readily available if only they knew how to gain access to it either directly or by asking those with different skills from their own. Librarians, to their great credit, are increasingly aware of this gap and of the need to cross it. Community information services, genuinely user-friendly public access information systems and the like, are some of the manifestations of this. Other agencies and professionals seem to be somewhat less aware of the problem, or are, perhaps, less willing to address the issues which it raises. In the UK, such documents as income tax returns and, most notoriously, the leaflets which allegedly 'explain' social security entitlements, became legendary for their obscurity, although this is now being remedied. Millions of pages of government information are available on the web, but its mere existence does not solve the problem. By bad presentation, or by failing to provide appropriate education and training, the state can deprive the citizen of information to which the state itself has determined that the citizen has a right of access. We shall return to this matter in Chapter 6.

Information poverty is a disadvantage when it deprives its victims of information which could be of benefit to them. Such benefits might be financial, professional, social, educational or purely a matter of personal convenience. It takes its place in the cycle of deprivation with other, more tangible, manifestations of poverty. Deprived of essential information, the citizen is deprived of the power of choice, because only informed choice can be rational choice. These consequences are, in many ways, analogous with the consequences of poor information infrastructures in the Third World or in eastern Europe. The information elites of the industrialized world are becoming ever more isolated from the excluded majorities, just as the economic gap between North and South is widening. There are, of course, exceptions; individuals can work their way into the elites, just as

countries can. Skill acquisition, through education or training, can change
the relationship between an individual and the information base of
society, just as Indonesia or Thailand can still hope to break through the
barriers to industrialized status. The obstacles, however, remain, and the
rate of enlargement of the elite is still small compared with the number of
those excluded.

The relationship between the information rich and the information
poor is the central political dilemma of the information society. Access to
information has become one of the points of conflict within and between
societies, and one of the measures of success and failure. The state has a
multifaceted role; it is, at the same time, the creator, owner and protector
of information, but also must try to encompass the interests of both the
information rich and the information poor. The next chapter explores
various aspects of this dilemma.

Chapter 6

Information, the state and the citizen

The value which can be assigned to information, both directly and indirectly, has done more than simply turn it into a commodity to be traded in the marketplace. There is some information which can never be the simple neutral object of a commercial transaction. Possessing it can bring too many benefits, and not possessing it too many disadvantages, for that to be possible. The creators of information are creating a piece of valuable property; sometimes it may be so valuable to the creator and possessor that it cannot be made generally available at all. These considerations underlie a complex and sometimes shadowy set of relationships between information itself, its creators, owners and providers, individual consumers or beneficiaries of information, and the apparatus of a state which seeks to regulate these interactions.

The role of the state: an introduction

In essence, the state can intervene in four ways between the information owner and the information-seeker. First, it can protect information as a piece of property in which the rights of ownership clearly belong to its legal possessor. This is the function of the law of copyright, and a number of associated forms of protection known to lawyers as 'adjacent rights' or, more generally, 'intellectual property'. Secondly, the state can prevent the unauthorized use of information that has been legitimately collected. This is the purpose of the growing body of law concerned with the protection of data, especially data on the personal and financial affairs of individuals. Thirdly, the state can guarantee the right of access to certain categories of information of concern, interest or benefit to its citizens. Freedom of information legislation works in several ways, but is normally concerned primarily with facilitating general access to information of general importance, while ensuring that individuals are aware of, and have some control over, data that concern them at a personal level. Finally, the state can prevent the dissemination of information. This can be for reasons of security, morality or political expediency, and can be overt or covert; it is, necessarily, the most difficult area to explore.

The role of the state: the protection of intellectual property

The need to afford some sort of protection to the owners of information was recognized for centuries before the concept would have been expressed in those terms. The distant origins of copyright lie in privileges granted by secular states and ecclesiastical authorities to individual printers and authors, the earliest examples of which are to be found in Italy and France before the end of the 15th century. There was a mixture of motives behind these grants. Some were intended to encourage the practitioners of the new and expensive craft of printing, perhaps because it was considered to be socially and culturally useful, or to have economic benefits. Some were intended to control the output of the press by limiting the numbers of printers and thereby making it easier to supervise their activities. In practice, these two approaches to the control and protection of the press became inextricably mixed. Censorship, in some form, was almost universal in early modern Europe, and it was out of the attempts to protect the state from the press that the book trade was able to develop the rights which allowed the state to afford the trade some protection.

In modern times, two traditions of copyright law have sometimes been identified, although in recent years there has been convergence between them. The British, or common law, tradition, which has been influential in the USA and throughout the English-speaking world, understands copyright as a piece of property which can be traded like any other commodity. The alternative Roman law tradition, which was first embodied in the *Code Napoléon*, and which influences the legal traditions of southern Europe and the Francophone and Hispanophone countries, regards copyright as a right which essentially belongs to the author, and over which the author retains 'moral rights', or *droit moral*, even after publication. The differences and conflicts between these traditions are not as marked as has sometimes been suggested, but they do represent different approaches to copyright as a concept. In the common law tradition, it is seen essentially as a commercial property, while the tradition deriving from the *Code Napoléon* emphasizes artistic integrity. In practice, however, the results are very similar. In both legal traditions, the primary purpose of copyright law is to ensure that those who are responsible for the creation and publication of a work have a reasonable opportunity to profit from it, and to prevent those who were not involved in the process from benefiting from the labours of others. Copyright law thus operates in two dimensions. On the one hand, it protects authors and publishers. It is the legal embodiment of the concept of information as property, and provides a mechanism for preventing the infringement of property rights; if prevention fails, it defines forms of punishment and prescribes penalties. On the other hand, copyright law regulates the circumstances under which copying and dissemination can legitimately happen.

Copyright normally takes the form of granting absolute protection to a newly created work for a fixed period of time. In many countries, this is now the author's lifetime and 50 years thereafter; in the European Union it is 70 years after death. During that time, the work can be reproduced only with the permission of the author (which may be a corporate body such as a company, a government department or a university) or the author's representatives. These representatives may be individuals or organizations to whom the rights have been sold or leased by the author. The function of the law in these commercial transactions between author and publisher is to provide the framework within which they can safely be conducted. The law of copyright protects the author's investment of intellectual effort and the publisher's investment of professional skill and risk capital. The same principle is extended to other areas of creative and intellectual activity. The law protects, in various ways, products as diverse as paintings and computer software, or indeed any original creation that is derived from the exercise of human imagination and skill. It also protects inventions through the different, but closely related, law of patents. Other rights which are protected include those in public performances of music or plays, and the public exhibition of movies. Even the images of sporting events can be protected under certain circumstances, thus allowing the activities of major sports and their major events (such as the Olympic Games) to be converted into broadcasting rights to the immense profits of the organisers and (in most cases) the broadcasters. The essence of the law is that the product may be reproduced, or in some cases used, only with the permission of the creator, thus giving that person (or corporate body) the opportunity to recoup their intellectual and perhaps financial investment.

Expressed in that way, the law of intellectual property seems neat and simple. In practice it is neither, partly because different manifestations of such property have to be treated in different ways. These arise from the inherent differences between the communication media which are used for information in different formats. The classic historical model of the copyright in a book has developed because of the printing and publishing process itself, with its heavy front-loaded investment of capital, and the author's partly conflicting desires both to disseminate the work and to protect it against dissemination by others. Illegally reprinting a book, however, is no easy matter, although it does happen, as we shall see. On the other hand, there are now technologies in which ease of copying and transmission are the very core of the information transfer process.

The most obvious of these is computing. The legal protection of computer software is fraught with problems. In current British law, under the Copyright (Computer Software) Amendment Act (1985) and the Copyright, Designs and Patent Act (1988), the position is that a computer program is as fully protected as if it were any other kind of intellectual property, such as a conventional written work. Similarly, the data stored in a database are protected on exactly the same basis, as are the design and structure of the database itself. This can lead to many complications. When a customer buys a copy of a computer program, such as a word-processing package, what is acquired is the right to use that copy only. The purchaser may not, for example, have the right to make a second copy of the program to use simultaneously on another computer. An important principle is embodied in this prohibition; the purchaser would not necessarily obtain direct financial benefit from the making of a second copy for personal use, but the owner of the rights in the program suffers the loss incurred by not selling a second copy. In fact, it is extremely difficult for the publishers of software to prevent such copying by private individuals, and they tend to concentrate their efforts on preventing illegal commercial exploitation of their products by the production and sale of pirated copies on a large scale. In addition, many software houses will grant so-called 'site licences', under which institutional purchasers (such as universities or companies) pay for the right to make a specified number of copies of a particular program for use on their premises for specific purposes or to run the software or database on their own network for internal use at a specified number of workstations. This is an invaluable compromise between unenforceable prohibitions and uncontrolled infringement of rights.

Intellectual property law is intended to be of benefit to both the creators and the users of information, by ensuring that the information market-place has a commercially sound basis. It achieves this by protecting the investment of the author and the publisher in the creation of the work and in its multiplication in a marketable format. Because the publisher acquires an effective monopoly of a particular work, it is possible to take the financial risk involved in making it available for sale and also to pay the author for the right to do so. The British tradition of regarding copyright as a commercial matter is exemplified in this approach. On the other hand, copyright and other intellectual property rights can sometimes operate to the apparent disadvantage of the user, and there is a need to maintain a balance between the interests of producers and those of the consumers whose demand creates the market which gives the product its commercial value in the first place. Two examples will illustrate this.

First, the law regulates the extent of photocopying of published material. Theoretically, all photocopying of copyright material is a breach of the general principle of copyright protection. In practice, technological developments have forced legislators to take a less extreme position. The concept of 'fair dealing', which is now embodied in the law in most industrialized countries, makes provision for limited amounts of photocopying for non-commercial purposes. These include private study, and, in certain circumstances, educational use. The law may also make provision (as the 1988 British law does) for licensing arrangements which facilitate the making of multiple photocopies for legitimate purposes, while ensuring that the copyright owners receive some financial compensation for the notional loss of sales which this entails.

There are, however, further issues to be considered. In the academic world, where most of the copying under the 'fair dealing' rules takes place, the principal concern is with copying papers in journals. When the fair dealing rules were first evolved in the late 1950s, it was argued that the publishers of such journals did not, in practice, suffer any loss by allowing limited copying for personal use, since it was considered to be highly improbable that the person making the copy would subscribe to the journal if copying were not permitted. The development of centralized document delivery services, however, has dealt a serious blow to this argument. Licensing arrangements may protect the publishers to some extent, and document delivery services are expected to be vigilant in upholding both the law in general and the fair dealing rules in particular, but lapses are inevitable. The publishers' interests were damaged by conventional, photocopy-based, document delivery services. Even greater damage is possible from network transmission of digitized images of documents (like those embodied in a PDF version of a printed journal), when the line between printed and electronic publication is no longer so clearly drawn.

It would be difficult to disprove the publishers' contention that large-scale document delivery services have had a deleterious effect on subscriptions, although their development has also coincided with a period of rising journal prices, an increased number of journal titles and a decline in the purchasing power of library budgets. The inevitable consequence has been to set up a vicious circle in which the easy availability of low-price document delivery services results in libraries cancelling subscriptions to periodicals which can be accessed through those services. As a result, the publishers must decrease the print run of the journal and increase its price, causing further loss of subscriptions and further price rises. This chain of events was already well advanced when the advent of the electronic journal almost rendered the issue obsolete. The publishers of electronic journals, as we saw in Chapter 4, can in effect license subscribers to access their database. Access, downloading and printing can all be regulated, and if necessary prevented in whole or in part, by the software controlled by the publisher. The potential for conflict between the needs of users and their ability to pay for information, on the one hand, and, on the other hand, the need for information providers to make a reasonable profit in order to sustain their continued activities, is only too clear. Publishers and information service providers (especially university libraries) are now recognizing the need to work together to resolve this conflict.

The conflict is essentially economic, but the second example of the difficulties that can arise out of copyright law has more overt cultural and educational implications. As we have suggested in Chapters 3 and 5, the information market-place is dominated by producers based in industrialized countries. More specifically, world publishing is dominated by the British and American publishers of books in the English language, who have an almost complete monopoly of high-level publishing in STM and academic publishing. The books and journals which they produce are necessarily expensive, sometimes even by western standards. Consequently, less developed countries have the utmost difficulty in obtaining such material. It is one of the more obvious ways in which cash poverty leads directly to information poverty. Publishers are not in business as aid agencies, but they do have some self-interest in trying to help the developing world to solve this dilemma. Again, technology lies at the root of the problem. It is often cheaper to make a photocopy of a book than it is to buy a copy of the book itself. For those who are remote from any likelihood of detection or punishment, the temptation may be irresistible. As with the photocopying of journal articles, however, the problem is not a serious one until it begins to interfere with legitimate trade. This happens if the illicit copies of a book are sold to those who would otherwise buy the original; the owner of the intellectual property is then clearly being deprived of rewards legitimated by the law.

Photocopying is a very crude and clumsy technology for mass copying for commercial purposes. There is, however, a far greater danger. Modern printing technology is also based on photographic systems. Photolithography, the system now in almost universal use, prints images from photographic plates which are both simple and relatively cheap to make. It is possible to make a plate from the page of a printed book without much greater difficulty than that involved in photocopying the same page. The issue has been further complicated by the advent of cheap and simple digital technology. A copy of a book can be digitized by a scanning device, and the output used either to generate plates or to print directly through a digital printing machine. This technology is used legitimately in the growing sector of Books on Demand (BOD) which gives publishers an economic means of keeping books available without having to finance expensive reprints. But it can also be put to illegitimate use. In both cases, the book will appear to be identical with the original. If identical paper is used, and an identical binding made, the deception will be complete. Such piracy (as this form of theft is rather romantically known) is common in some parts of the world; in some NICs it represents a substantial part of the work of sophisticated printing industries. For western publishers, piracy is a very serious problem. The success of the piratical reprints of English-language books of all kinds, from popular fiction to STM monographs and school textbooks, demonstrates the existence of a market for such books. Yet it is one which the original publishers themselves cannot aspire to reach; their prices are too high, for they are locked into the high-cost economics which dominate the book production industry in the industrialized world. Moreover, western governments have not been entirely unsympathetic to the complaints of the governments of developing countries that the high price of essential educational and scientific books is actually hindering development by inhibiting education and research. It was out of such arguments that the idea was developed of licensing reprints in developing countries for domestic use in those countries.

Since the late 19th century, copyright law, and indeed all law relating to intellectual property, has been steadily internationalized. Ideas are no respecters of international political boundaries, and the books and other information media which carry them are just as difficult to restrict. The basic principle of international copyright law is very simple: all books, regardless of their 'national' origin, are as fully protected in any country as if they had originated there. The practice is embodied in two major conventions which are the basis of international copyright law. These are the Berne Convention, originally signed in 1886 but subsequently much modified, and the Universal Copyright Convention (UCC), signed in 1952 and, like Berne, subject to subsequent modifications. Although the two conventions have some important differences of approach, in fact most countries are signatories of both, and both incorporate the essential principle of reciprocity, Berne somewhat more strictly than UCC. It was in revising the Berne Convention in the late 1960s and early 1970s that the problem of book availability in the developing countries was firmly addressed.

The technical and legal details need not concern us. The important point is that the Paris Act (sometimes referred to as the 'Paris Amendments') modified the Berne Convention by introducing the principle that developing countries should have special privileges and rights in relation to the reprinting of copyright materials needed for educational and developmental purposes. In essence, a publisher in a developing country can apply to a western publisher for a licence to reprint a title in which that publisher holds the rights, and the western publisher is obliged to grant the licence without charge. There are, however, two essential conditions: the reprint is for domestic use in the producer country and not for export, and the work must be intended for educational purposes. In other words, the Paris Act was an attempt to solve the problem of the supply of essential, but necessarily very expensive, western books to the developing world. There is some evidence that it has indeed had this effect.

These two examples of the workings of copyright law - the photocopying of journal articles and the reprinting of western books elsewhere in the world - illustrate how it can inhibit the dissemination of information. This inhibition is not, of course, accidental. The whole point of protecting intellectual property of any kind is to ensure that it is disseminated in a way which benefits its creators and protects their interests. The difficulties arise when this legitimate desire to protect property comes into conflict with the equally legitimate needs of potential beneficiaries. The decisions to be taken in resolving this conflict are political rather than professional. The protection afforded by patents, for example, is, for all practical purposes, absolute. Like computer software, the use of a patent may be licensed to named producers (as often happens in the pharmaceutical industry, for example) but the rights clearly remain with their original owner, or, in rare cases, outright purchaser.

Intellectual property law is, in effect, the regulator of the information market-place, determining the conditions under which trading is conducted there. Like any regulatory mechanism, it is both inhibitory and permissive. It is generally, however, intended to stimulate the information transfer process by protecting the financial and intellectual interests of those who have created information products of any kind. The very concept is an extension beyond the usual limits of the law of property, where the state normally intervenes only to protect the owner against infringements of what is rightfully owned. In dealing with intellectual property, the law makes the assumption, which we have detected elsewhere, that information is so important that its owners and those responsible for its commercial dissemination must be afforded some additional protection. Originally this concept was, perhaps, not dissimilar from the 'cultural' case for regulating book prices discussed in Chapter 4.

From the middle of the 18th century onwards, authors were increasingly aware of their 'rights' and of their role in the creation of commercially valuable products. Gradually, these rights were recognized by the law and incorporated into it. Different traditions produced different results. In Britain, from 1842 to 1988, the law essentially recognized the author as a partner in a series of commercial transactions; French law (and the American Constitution) broadened this understanding to include the author's 'moral right' to protect the artistic integrity of the work. In 1988, this concept was at last incorporated into British law. Authors now retain moral rights in the work, and can forbid it to be used or altered in ways of which they do not approve. The law, like the society of which it is a product, sees artistic and literary works, and especially perhaps books, as being, in some ill defined but nevertheless broadly accepted way, 'different'.

We should not, however, focus entirely on print products. All stored information is protected by copyright, including the digital data which are the basis of audio and video recordings and material which is made available through the internet and the world wide web. For most of the 20th century, information technology changed so quickly that the law was unable to keep up with it. In the 1911 Copyright Act in the UK, for example, there was some protection for sound recordings and cinema films; but there was nothing about broadcasting until the 1956 Act, and even that focused on radio rather than television. Before there was another major revision of the law (in 1988) the media had changed beyond recognition. The 1988 Act is now the framework for the world of networked computing and instantaneous transmission, downloading, copying and redistribution of unprecedented quantities of information. At the same time, the copying technologies have also become cheap and simple, developing from the reel-to-reel tape recorders which became commercially available in the early 1950s to the devices which can now be used for downloading, storing and reproducing music and video from the internet. As we shall see in the last section of this chapter, the whole concept of intellectual property as it was understood in the age of print is now under threat.

The role of the state: data protection and personal privacy

It could be argued that there is a fundamental ambiguity in the modern approach to intellectual property law: on the one hand, it seeks to facilitate the operation of the market-place, while, on the other, it seeks to protect the integrity of some of the products made for that market-place. A similar ambiguity, resulting perhaps from the sheer complexity of the subject, can be seen when we turn to an even more contentious subject: the state's role in the storage, use and regulation of personal data.

The protection of personal data is not a new issue, but it is one which, in its contemporary form, is closely linked to the evolution of computing and the ever-increasing use of the computer by governments, institutions and businesses. Vast quantities of data are collected for perfectly legitimate purposes. In an industrialized country, for example, various agencies of the state hold information about the nationality, age, marital status, family circumstances, income, health and place of residence of individuals. These are collected for such purposes as assessing and collecting taxes, issuing passports, ensuring the right to vote, providing welfare benefits and recording the obligation to undertake such duties as serving on a jury or performing a period of compulsory military service. In other words, the state collects the information which is needed to ensure that its citizens fulfil their obligations and receive their entitlements. No modern state could function without such information. Computers have transformed the efficiency and comprehensiveness of the processes of collecting, sorting and using the data, but not their fundamental purpose.

It is not, however, only governments that hold information about individuals. A great deal is held by other public or semi-public bodies. Local or regional governments (depending upon the constitutional arrangements in force in particular countries) may hold some or all of the information also held by central governments. In the USA, for example, some states have their own income taxes, which means that they, as well as the federal government, hold information relating to personal and corporate incomes. In Britain, information about the value of property is held by local authorities for whom it is the basis of their calculation of the tax obligations of residents and property owners. However, information is also held by many non-governmental public sector bodies, such as schools, universities and hospitals and other health-care agencies. Unlike central and local government, these bodies are not usually directly accountable through a democratically elected representative body to those about whom the information is held.

In the private sector, there is no visible accountability, and yet the amount of information held is vast. It includes some which is of great personal sensitivity, such as financial data, data which record personal expenditure, travel arrangements and similar private activities. The largest sets of these records are, in a sense, created accidentally. Credit-card transactions are usually automated from the moment they take place, through online links to the card-issuer's computer which checks the state of the cardholder's account. Even in the rare instances when the actual transaction is manual, the credit company will eventually create a computer-held record which will calculate interest payments, issue invoices, record payments, and so on. All this is innocuous, and beneficial to the user of the service that the company provides. The records that are created, however, have a vast potential for misuse because of the records of expenditure which they create. Moreover, because credit transactions have become such an important element in the pattern of personal expenditure in most

industrialized countries, agencies have been established which collect such
data and use them to establish a credit rating for individuals. On this basis,
a person may be refused further credit, not merely by a company with
which he or she already has an account, but by another agency for a quite
different purpose. Credit rating agencies are regulated, and banks and other
financial institutions are bound by legal as well as professional requirements
of secrecy and confidentiality. Nevertheless, there is a growing body of
evidence of abuse of the credit rating system, as well as inevitable errors
which can seriously disadvantage an individual or even devastate a
business. The accidental loss of data – or more often of portable media – is
a particular concern. There have been several well publicized incidents in
which CD-ROMs and indeed laptops with sensitive data have been lost or
stolen. Data owners are of course responsible for this, and may even be
legally liable for the consequences to data subjects. But that is little comfort
to the ultimate victims whose privacy – and worse – has been jeopardized.

Even more insidious, and a matter of growing concern, is the issue of
identity theft. The use of stolen credit cards has perhaps been diminished
by the widespread adoption of Chip and PIN systems, but PINs can also
be stolen, and there are devices which can copy cards at ATMs in public
places. A thief needs little more than a name and address to establish a
line of credit; a stolen passport or driving licence, or even a utility bill or
in extreme cases the label from an envelope or parcel, can become a
powerful criminal weapon. The growth of e-commerce – the use of the
internet for buying and selling – has also opened up new fields for
criminal as well as legitimate activity. Online purchasing of everything
from CDs to groceries has been one of growth areas of the last decade.
Responsible retailers of course have high levels of data security built into
their systems. But the motto 'buyer beware' was never more appropriate
than in dealing with an unknown provider.

The whole area exposes the power of information at its most
dangerous. Much of this information was being sought and held by public
and private bodies long before computers were commonly available. The
use of computers, however, has raised new concerns for two reasons.
First, computers can sort data far more quickly than was ever possible in
a manual system. The ability to process and retrieve the raw data is the

real basis of the information holder's power over those who are the subjects of the information. Secondly, because data can be exchanged electronically between computers without significant human intervention, they can also easily be exchanged between databases and thus between agencies. It is, for example, perfectly possible, in a technical sense, to compare data relating to income tax, social security payments and property values for a single individual by combining data from files held by different central and local government departments. To restrict the almost unlimited power of information holders, the state has intervened to regulate the ways in which data can be collected, stored, exchanged and used even by its own constituent parts.

This has become a very complex area of state intervention in the information field. Most industrialized countries developed data protection legislation of some kind during the 1970s and 1980s; in Britain, it was embodied in the Data Protection Act of 1984, but this was a comparative latecomer to the field. Some of the German *Land* governments have had such legislation since the early 1970s, and throughout that decade the issue was a matter of growing concern in the Council of Europe, the Organization for Economic Cooperation and Development, the Commission of the European Community and UNESCO. Gradually, some generally accepted principles have developed, on the basis of which national legislation and international agreements have brought some order to a potentially chaotic field. The guiding principle of data protection in the democracies is that information should be used only for the purpose for which it is gathered, and that the subject of the information should have the right to be certain of its accuracy and relevance. The basic principles are embodied in laws which differ between jurisdictions; the principles themselves now seem to be fairly common.

In practice, however, the law is often less effective than it was intended to be; moreover, because of the very nature of the subject there is inevitable suspicion about its operation. In British law, as revised in 1998 to extend protection to manual files as well as automated databases, all owners of files that contain personal information about identifiable individuals are required to register with an agency (originally the Data Protection Registry, but now the Information Commission) established for the purpose. When information is included in a registered database (unregistered databases are illegal), the subjects of the information have the right of access, to assure themselves that the information is correct, up to date and complete. There is, however, a large number of exceptions to the general rule, most of which are designed to protect the state rather than the individual. Quite apart from the inevitable, and inevitably vague, provision that data considered vital to national security are exempt, there are also exemptions for data collected for the detection and prosecution of alleged criminals, and the assessment of taxes.

The real purpose of data protection law is, or should be, not the protection of the state, but the protection of the individual. Registered holders of data may use them only for the purpose for which they have been collected, and may not disclose them to third parties without the permission of the data subject. The importance of this in the case of medical or financial information is obvious. On the other hand, data subjects can give permission for information to be disclosed under certain circumstances. Those whose names appear on mailing lists, for example, can give the owner of the mailing list the right to disclose it to other persons or bodies. This is normally a commercial transaction, and indeed buying and selling mailing lists has become a large-scale business in its own right. This is especially true of mail-order companies and of agencies who use direct mail shots for advertising. Where the presence of a name on a mailing list (for example, of a credit card company) implies something about economic status and spending habits, the sellers of goods and services aimed at that sector of society can obviously benefit from being able to target their marketing comparatively narrowly. Moreover, it is, in practice, necessary for data subjects to ask that their names are omitted or removed from a mailing list before it is sold, rather than to ask that they shall be included. As a result, there was a great increase in direct mail-order businesses in Britain in the 1990s, especially for comparatively high-profit goods such as wine, or profitable services such as insurance. The computerized mailing list has all but displaced the traditional door-to-door salesman as a direct-selling mechanism to the home; e-commerce is completing the process.

Direct sales based on computer-held mailing lists may be seen simply as a nuisance which increases the volume of junk mail (including junk e-mail) and, coincidentally, the profits of the postal and telecommunications services and the ISPs. Other uses of data are, however, more insidious. Agencies which hold data that are used to determine the creditworthiness of an individual or company are carefully regulated by law, but there have been examples of inaccurate or out-of-date information held by such an agency being used to the detriment of the data subject. It is a murky area, about which little hard evidence is available; consumer organizations, investigative journalists and consumer-oriented radio and television programmes are among those who monitor it, perhaps more effectively than the law and the state.

The issues that surround personal data held in computer databases highlight the fact that the use of computers has not been a universal and unadulterated benefit. The human ingenuity that produced computers in the first place can be applied to their misuse as well as their use. Personal data have come to have a high commercial value. Information, whether or not it is legitimately obtained or legally stored, is important for individuals and for businesses. The law has tried to afford some protection against abuse, but protection is often difficult to enforce. The potential financial rewards are substantial, and as a result data abuse, and even theft, has become one of the seamier sides of the information society.

The role of the state: freedom of information

Data protection law generally embodies, as it does in the UK, provisions giving data subjects the right of access to information about them. There is also, however, a much broader issue concerning access to information and the 'right' of the citizen to be informed by the state. The role of the state in the circulation and storage of information is not confined to regulation. A modern state itself generates information on a massive scale, some of it for its own purposes and some for public consumption. It seeks to conceal information whose publication is perceived to be to its disadvantage, while disseminating that which is regarded as beneficial to its interests. Governments have, as we have suggested, always held huge amounts of information. The advent of computers has greatly increased the store of such information, and also, in principle, made access to it easier. The practice, however, is somewhat different.

Governments collect information through a multitude of channels. At the most basic level, almost all countries conduct a population census at regular intervals, typically decennially. The census is designed primarily to enumerate the population, but with modern data-processing methods it can also collect a great deal of other data, which can be stored, sorted and analysed for a wide variety of purposes. This might include information on such matters as occupation, educational attainments, housing conditions, religious affiliations, ethnic origins, and so on. In the UK, as in other democracies, information collected for census purposes is not published in a form which allows it to be attributed to individuals, and the documents on which the returns are made are treated as confidential for a long time (in Britain, 100 years) after the date of the census itself. After analysis, however, the anonymized data are published, and can be used for matters as diverse as academic research in sociology or the planning of transport systems.

The census provides the basic statistical data for the state, but yet more information is needed for it to function efficiently. In all democracies, there is a process of voter registration, which identifies and lists those with the right to vote in particular elections. Typically, this is a section of the population defined by age, citizenship and residence. Voter registration takes place at more frequent intervals than a full census. In the UK, it is an annual process; in some other countries, including the USA, it immediately precedes an election or is part of the electoral process itself. In any case, the resulting lists are normally published and available for verification by those whose names appear on them or are wrongly omitted from them. In contrast to the census data, voter registration data are, by definition, in the public domain, and can therefore be legitimately used for many purposes. Their most obvious use is by the political parties for their own purposes such as campaigning, but they can also be exploited by commercial organizations, mail-order companies, advertisers and the like. The growing use of the register for commercial purposes led to new British legislation in 2000. The Parties, Elections and Referendums

Act of that year established the Electoral Commission to have oversight of registration and associated processes and products. One immediate change was the creation of two parallel electoral registers; the full register is a complete list of voters, but there is also an edited register from which electors can choose to withhold their names. Only the edited register can lawfully be used for commercial purposes, thus protecting individuals from junk mail and other unsolicited commercial activities, as well as from another roll which can be used in fraud and identity theft.

Both the census and the electoral register contain information collected comprehensively for public use, of which the results and some of the details will, eventually, be in the public domain. The state, however, also collects or accumulates a vast amount of data on individuals, which become a matter of record but are nevertheless treated as being wholly or partly confidential. Information relating to personal and corporate incomes, gathered for taxation purposes, is the most obvious example of private information which the state requires of the citizen. In the UK (although not in all countries, most notably not in the USA), income tax data is treated as being confidential between the taxation authority itself and the individual to whom the information relates. Any dissemination of the information is at the request of the individual (to an accountant, for example), except in extreme circumstances, such as when a court investigates alleged offences in relation to the payment (or non-payment) of tax, or illegal activities such as money laundering or foreign exchange transactions especially in relation to dealings thought to involve armaments or unlawful drugs.

Company taxation information is treated differently. British companies are required by law to register their existence on a register kept at Companies House; this register, which contains basic data about the company, including its ownership and management, is open to inspection. Similar arrangements prevail in most other industrialized countries. In the case of public limited companies in the UK, they must also publish to their shareholders annual statements of their financial affairs. In that sense, the accounts (and hence, for example, the tax liabilities) of public companies are a matter of public record. Companies, however, have the same rights as individuals to privacy about much of their financial business, such as the operation of their bank accounts.

The precise nature of the information collected from or about individuals for tax purposes varies according to the nature of the direct taxation process. The taxation of income is the norm in almost all countries, with the employer usually involved in the process by deducting the tax due from an employee's salary before it is paid. The employer, however, knows nothing of any income which an employee may derive from other sources such as investments. Other forms of direct taxation also require the collection and storage of information. Property taxes are common in most countries. This necessitates the maintenance of a register both of property and of property ownership or occupation. Confidentiality rules vary from country to country. Other forms of revenue generation by the state, whether for general or specific purposes, are also dependent on the availability of accurate information. Social security contributions are usually income related, as in the UK; these too are often deducted from earned income at source. Moreover, in almost all countries the social security system identifies individuals by a unique number, which they carry throughout their lives. In Britain and the USA, these registers compiled for social security purposes are the nearest approach to a national system of registration and identification of citizens.

In neither country is there any formal system of identity (ID) cards, although this is common in almost all other democracies and in virtually every state which is not democratic. In both the UK and the USA, however, the use of some form of ID is becoming increasingly common. In the USA, social security cards and driving licences have been used as *de facto* ID cards for many years. In the UK, where until recently driving licences did not carry a photograph, heightened awareness of security issues has led to the demand for photographic ID in many circumstances and opened a debate about moving towards ID cards on the continental European model. Public distrust of the government's ability to maintain the highest levels of data security seems likely to be a factor in the ongoing debate. In most countries, everyone is required to carry an identity card at all times, and to show it to authorized officials on request. An extension of the principle of the ID card is the passport, which identifies its holder for the purposes of international travel. Indeed, passports are being used for some domestic purposes in

Britain in the absence of ID cards; perhaps the most familiar example is the requirement of airlines that passengers on domestic flights can show some form of photographic ID (of which a driving licence or a passport is the most obvious example) before boarding a flight.

The information collected by registration and passport issuing agencies represents another vast data set held by the state which records information about its citizens. This by no means exhausts the list of such data. Records of driving licences and vehicle registration and taxation are increasingly comprehensive. Britain's unique system of funding its public broadcasting system creates another almost universal listing of householders in the records of the issue of television licences. All of this provides the state with a comprehensive and potentially very valuable record of the existence, location, financial affairs and activities of its citizens.

Information about individuals is collected by the state for its own administrative purposes, and in democracies its use is carefully regulated by law. In general, the overarching principles of data protection apply: there is a right of verification, and information can be used only for the purposes for which it is obtained unless with the prior permission of the data subject. In practice, restraints on the state tend to be less strict than those on the private owners of databases. Moreover, abuses of the system do inevitably occur, whether by design or through error or folly. Almost all of the data collected by the state are stored in electronic databases, and no computer system is wholly immune from unauthorized access. In addition, concern is expressed from time to time that data collected for legitimate purposes are collated for reasons of security or surveillance of individuals or organizations thought to present a threat to the state. This is a problematic area, both in law and in practice, about which there is, inevitably, much speculation but little hard information. Certainly, even democratic states can be presumed to hold some data about individual citizens which have not been collected with their participation or consent. In Britain, criminal records and other non-criminal information is kept on the National Criminal Information System; for reasons thought to be obvious, this is not open to public scrutiny and its records cannot therefore be validated by the data subjects. This inevitably arouses suspicion among those concerned with civil liberties and human rights.

Governments, however, do not confine their data collection activities to individuals. For purposes of registration, taxation and regulation they also collect a great deal of information about businesses, both individually and collectively. Much of this is of great political and economic significance, providing, as it does, the statistical basis for an analysis of the functioning of the economy. Both national governments, and supranational agencies like the European Union, publish huge economic data sets at regular intervals; these inform economic planning at every level down to that of the small business. Indeed, the provision of information to businesses, especially in the critical early stages of their development, is regarded as an important function of government and its information agencies.

Social and economic information collected and processed by the state or by international agencies is essentially a planning tool. It shows the role of the state as a benevolent participant in the process of information gathering and dissemination, and fulfilling its function of assisting individuals and organizations to realize their full economic potential, and hence benefit the state as a whole. There are, however, some very real problems inherent in the vast amount of data that are generated. Even information professionals can become entangled in the jungle thickets of official documents, especially those from international bodies, and for individuals these thickets are all but impenetrable. Increasingly, therefore, governments and international bodies have established information agencies through which the information that they generate and publish can be made accessible to its potential beneficiaries.

The European Union has been active in this respect, with its European Documentation Centres and European Information Centres, often based on existing public sector library services. The pattern was established 50 years ago by some of the United Nations agencies, especially UNESCO with its National Commissions, intended to make its work and its publications better known in member states. At national level in Britain, steps have been taken towards making government information easier to use. The development of comprehensive government websites is a major advance, and at a regional level, many local authorities have established 'information shops' and similar agencies, as well as websites, often bypassing their own library service, through which businesses and individuals can gain access to, and take advantage of, the information which has been published and which it is their right to use. There is a policy objective of achieving web access to all government document-ation; there are thousands of .gov.uk websites, and they are increasingly used both for information and to conduct transactions such as making income tax returns or taxing motor vehicles. So far as the informational sites are concerned, there is a major issue here: the state is an active producer of information but, like all information providers, it is perhaps in danger of overwhelming the end-user.

The information collected and held by the state about its citizens and their activities, both social and economic, is one of the most potent manifestations of the information society. The state itself has become a generator, user and provider of information, and at the same time has become dependent upon it. In democracies, the use of this power is regulated by laws, some of which we have briefly explored in this chapter. Information relating to the private affairs of individuals is protected whether it is held publicly or privately with the consent of the data subject. Some publicly held information, such as the electoral register, is necessarily in the public domain, but that is explicit in the law under which it is collected and processed. In general, however, there is probably more concern about the misuse or abuse of information by the state than there is about lack of privacy. There are two approaches to this, the third area of state and legal involvement in information (as described on pages 133–4), which differ radically, and are perhaps best exemplified by the differences in attitude shown in the laws of the UK and the USA.

British law has always been based on the assumption that all information gathered or generated by the state is secret, and need only be revealed if this is a legal requirement. In general, the burden of proof in disputed cases rests with those seeking the information, who have to show that they need it for some proper purpose. All documents generated by government and its agencies are closed for 30 years, after which time those deposited in the Public Record Office for archival preservation are made available. There are, however, substantial exceptions even to this rule. Some documents are protected for 100 years or even in perpetuity. Civil servants and others who reveal information from government documents within the 30-year embargo period may be guilty of a criminal offence, as may those, principally journalists or publishers, who publish or disseminate any document or information which is revealed. In other words, British law, primarily concerned with protecting the security of the state, is based upon a presumption of secrecy. This is embodied by the principal piece of legislation upon which the law in this field depends: the Official Secrets Act.

The current (1989) version of the Official Secrets Act was intended both to simplify and to clarify the ambiguities in its predecessors of 1911 and 1920. It remains the case, however, that it fundamentally inhibits the communication, publication or dissemination of information generated or collected by the state and its agencies. Few would question that some of this information is legitimately restricted in the interests of national security; this might include, for example, information relating to defence establishments and weapons systems, or information assembled about the covert agents of foreign states operating in the UK. The problem is that the Act, like all secret systems, is open not only to abuse but also to the suspicion of abuse. The Act does allow a defence of 'public interest', under which a person accused of an offence can argue that the disclosure of information was for the general good. This defence has been successfully used by civil servants and others, but the Act remains unpopular in many quarters. Further reform was on the political agenda before 2001, but now seems unlikely.

Even in Britain, there are exceptions to blanket secrecy about the activities of government. The proceedings of Parliament and of local councils are, with a few exceptions, conducted in public, and both the proceedings themselves, and the background papers which facilitate the business, are in the public domain. At local government level, the minutes and papers of committee meetings, through which the detailed business of councils is actually conducted, are also public, but, at national level, what might be thought to be comparable documents, such as the minutes and papers of the Cabinet and its committees, are protected under the 30-year rule. In general, however, the law, especially the Local Government (Access to Information) Act of 1985, carefully regulates what must be made available, while continuing to assume that everything else is secret. The United Kingdom was very slow in developing legislation in this field.

From 1979 to 1997, there was a government which resolutely refused to act on the matter. The Freedom of Information Act, which was finally passed in 2000, took five years to implement in full, but there is now growing evidence of its effectiveness. Journalists and even MPs have made good use of it to prise out information which government and other authorities would prefer not to have put into the public domain. Crucially, the enforcement of the Act is linked to the enforcement of the Data Protection Act, with the Information Commission having ultimate responsibility for both. The critical test, however, will be whether the ingrained culture of secrecy in British government will change; early indications are not uniformly encouraging, not least because security is so often invoked as a reason for not making information available.

A very different attitude has prevailed in the USA. The Freedom of Information Act of 1975 effectively put all federal government information and documents into the public domain, unless the government could prove that national security was endangered by publication. This approach is diametrically opposite to that in the UK, although it is not an unmixed blessing. When the Act was first passed, some journalists in Washington complained that the government was providing so much information that they were unable to cope with it and that they had been able to work more efficiently when they had to ferret out for themselves what they needed to know! Nevertheless, the distinction between the two approaches exemplifies two differing views of the relationship between the state and its own citizens. Moreover, there are suggestions that this approach is being challenged even in the USA, under the guise of responding to the threat of terrorism. Intellectual property, data protection and freedom of information all exemplify different aspects of the three-way relationship between information itself, the state and the individual citizen. In each of these cases, the role of the state has been to intervene in the chain of communication between the source and the user of information. Almost inevitably such intervention is inhibitory. The stimulatory role of intellectual property law, in encouraging the publishers of books, the owners of databases, the creators of patents and others to continue to develop such products, is a coincidental benefit and a *post facto* justification of a law designed essentially to protect the interests of authors and publishers in their capacity as the owners of property. Data protection legislation, although designed to protect individuals from unwarranted intrusion on their privacy, can, in practice, be used for commercial purposes which do involve some such intrusion, however trivial it may be thought to be. Freedom of information is the least widely understood and the least developed area of the three. This is significant, for freedom of information can only be beneficial to citizens if it is considered that a well informed citizen derives benefits from the information that is acquired. The state, and those who constitute its government and bureaucracy, is exposed whenever there is open access to information.

The role of the state: censorship

The fourth and final major area of state intervention in the communication chain is the oldest of all: censorship. The concept is a familiar one, and has been so for centuries. The state seeks to prevent the publication or dissemination of information and opinion which it considers to be detrimental to its own understanding of its interests. The nature of the perceived detriment may vary. In early modern Europe, for example, Catholic and Protestant authorities censored each other's religious writings on grounds which were both moral and political. In some Islamic countries it is illegal to sell or distribute the Bible, as it was in some of the former socialist countries in eastern Europe. Overt political censorship has significantly diminished since 1989, but in many developing countries opposition newspapers have great difficulty in surviving, partly because governments can and do prevent their circulation, but, more insidiously, because pro-government newspapers are heavily subsidized, receive favourable treatment from government and are more widely available at more affordable prices.

Censorship of the printed word has, however, become significantly more difficult as a result of modern technological developments. During the 1991 attempted *coup d'état* in what was then still the Soviet Union, the anti-coup forces kept their allies in other parts of the country informed by using fax connections which had not, in an act of incredible folly and oversight, been cut. Indeed, for much of the last 20 years of its existence, the Soviet state was severely undermined by one technology after another. Photocopying, and even duplicating machines, made possible the production of underground literature on a small but significant scale, with far less risk of detection than would have been incurred by using conventional printing equipment, even if that had been available. Short-wave radio broadcasts, some overtly propagandist (such as Voice of America or Radio Free Europe) and one or two merely objective (most notably the BBC World Service), overcame some of the ignorance created by media wholly owned and controlled by the state. Towards the very end, the growing ease of international telecommunications, fax and e-mail ate yet further into the decaying fabric of the Soviet state. In the last months of European communism, the availability of news through satellite television created a 'copycat' movement which destabilized one regime after another from Germany to Siberia. State communism in eastern Europe was not destroyed by information technology, but it is clear from the experience of those countries that the new technologies of information and communication made it difficult and finally impossible for governments to continue to exercise untrammelled control over the dissemination of information in comparatively advanced societies.

Not for the first time, however, we confront a technological paradox; the very developments that have made censorship more difficult have also made it easier. As we have seen, most information about current affairs comes from television and radio, not from newspapers. Those media are comparatively easy for the state to control. In some countries, the state is indeed the monopoly owner of broadcasting systems but, even where a more or less free market prevails, there are still some controls. The most important is economic, for the capital costs of television broadcasting are still astronomically high. Competition is possible, and has been achieved in most industrialized countries, but it is only between very large companies, and it is comparatively limited in scope. Even in the USA, which probably has the least regulated television industry in the world, licences to broadcast are granted on a regional basis, and some restrictions are placed on the extent of competition permitted between companies. At the same time, however, technology has made the regulation of broadcasting more difficult. Satellite television is, by its very nature, international and there is evidence that satellite news broadcasters have actually influenced the development of events in some countries by making information available to their citizens which national broadcasters were forced to suppress. The development of cheap and easily portable digital video cameras has also been a significant factor in subverting or circumventing censorship.

Even more recent developments have also opened up new channels for dissemination. Key sites on the social web, such as YouTube and Facebook, have given individuals the power to disseminate whatever information they choose. Although for the most part this power is used for comparatively trivial personal and social purposes, there is already evidence of the use of such sites for the dissemination of information and images which a government would prefer to suppress. There have been instances of such activities in Afghanistan, Pakistan and Kenya in 2007 and 2008, comparable perhaps with the use of blogs by residents in Baghdad and elsewhere to offer an alternative version of the events after the American invasion of Iraq.

The high capital costs of entering the information market-place are only one way in which technology can help a censor. Telecommunications links are as vital to links between computers as they are to conventional telephone connections. Whether fixed or mobile, these are also normally the subject of complex regulatory regimes, in which the state plays a major role either as regulator or as active participant. Just as the information poor are excluded from many of the benefits of the information technology revolution, so some of the information rich may have their benefits restricted by the control which the state can exercise over their access to communications systems.

There is, however, a great difference between regulation of communications systems, which could be argued to be the only way to maintain a comprehensive and orderly service, and overt interference with the information and opinion which is disseminated through those systems. In many western countries, most notably the USA, the freedom of the press is the subject of legal or constitutional guarantees. Like freedom of information, however, freedom of the press is a fine phrase and an attractive idea, but it has sometimes proved rather less easy to implement as a practical policy.

Total freedom to publish and disseminate without control of any kind has never been institutionalized, although it may occasionally have happened in revolutionary situations from England in 1642 to Russia in 1991. The freedom of the press is limited both economically and legally. The legal restrictions vary immensely but, even at their lightest, they include some limitations on the publication of defamatory statements about individuals, and usually on the publication of material deemed to be morally objectionable. Both of these areas are even more difficult to define than overt political censorship, but both represent serious inhibitions on the free communication of information. The understanding of defamation varies in different legal systems. In the USA, for example, a true statement cannot normally be libellous, whereas the key British criterion is whether the subject's reputation is damaged. Indeed, libel is an area in which participants in public life in Britain are exceptionally litigious, often making use of such devices as an injunction under which a court can forbid the publication of information until there is time to hold a full trial which will determine whether or not it is defamatory or otherwise unlawful. The laws of libel are a formidable obstacle to a free press, and are open to abuse by the unscrupulous. The late James Goldsmith was a master of the art of using the law in this way to protect his reputation and to attack his enemies during his lifetime; even in Britain, however, the libel laws do not protect the dead.

Moral censorship rests on even less certain foundations. Both secular states such as the USA and France, as well as secularized societies like the UK, still retain legislation which attempts to prescribe the acceptable moral limits of publication in many formats. The pre-distribution censorship of films in all formats and through all media is commonplace even in the democracies. In practice, many film producers, like the television production companies and distribution networks in many countries, exercise a form of self-censorship in order to keep within the boundaries of the law and what is socially acceptable. Moral censorship of printed matter is even more difficult, although pre-publication censorship, equivalent to the pre-release classification of movies and DVDs, is not normally practised in democratic states. In Britain, the 1959 Obscene Publications Act turned juries into literary critics by requiring them to determine whether or not a work had 'literary merit', for, if it had, it was less likely to fall within the scope of the law. Like similar legislation elsewhere, the Act has brought the law into disrepute and ridicule, without seriously inhibiting the illicit publication of the pornography at which it was, presumably, aimed.

The internet has opened up a whole new field of debate about moral censorship. There are websites which are the electronic equivalent of pornographic magazines, and these have perhaps emphasized the difficulty of defining what is acceptable. Images which can be openly sold in newsagents' shops (however distasteful) can hardly be prevented from appearing on the web. But the internet also provides a channel for clearly illegal material (pornographic images of children being the most obvious example), and it is generally agreed that it is inappropriate to use publicly supported networks (such as SuperJANET) to access such material for non-academic purposes. In practice, blanket regulation is all but impossible without a politically unacceptable level of intervention in the operation of the internet, but codes of conduct have been developed by service providers with sanctions (such as denial of access) against 'offenders'. In the absence of state control – whether because it is impossible or because it is politically unacceptable – software has been developed both by internet service providers and by cable and satellite broadcasters which allows parents to control their children's surfing and viewing. How effective this is in practice, it is impossible to judge.

Moral censorship, like the other matters discussed in this chapter, represents an aspect of the state's role in the communication of information. It is inevitable that the state should have such a role. It is in the very nature of the information society that vast quantities of information are stored and are theoretically available. The state, at the very least, has a duty to its citizens to protect them against the abuse of that stored information. At the same time, the state, on behalf of its citizens, has an interest in ensuring that the channels of information and communications can operate effectively. The difficulty is the cost of maintaining them. The infrastructure of inform-ation supply, through whatever medium, is now so expensive that without some form of protection it is doubtful whether it could exist at all. This consideration is the ultimate justification for intellectual property laws, especially in relation to copyright, and for state intevention in the regulation of telecommunications and broadcasting.

Contemporary dilemmas: the issues redefined

If we take this comparatively benevolent view of the role of the state, we can see both data protection and freedom of information legislation, where they exist, as being manifestations of a liberal state protecting its citizens. Both are designed to ensure that citizens are well informed about those matters which they have a right to know, while simultaneously protecting their personal privacy. The problem, which has been implicit throughout this chapter, is in defining the limits of the public and the private domain; it is an issue which arises frequently in the so called 'public interest' defence against charges of breaches of official secrecy and state security. If the state is merely the corporate embodiment of its citizens, and exists solely to represent their interests and their collective will, then it could be argued that the right to know is absolute, and that the state, as in the American system, must be able to justify depriving citizens of any information of which it itself is possessed. In practice, the rights of individuals are generally far more limited than this position implies.

These issues have always been important in the democracies, for they concern the very nature of the democratic process itself. It could be argued that information lies at the heart of that process, on the grounds that only an informed citizen can cast an informed vote. On the other hand, the state also has a protective role in relation to its citizens. There is general agreement that this includes protecting the state itself against its external and internal enemies, and that this must certainly influence its policies towards the provision and concealment of information. There is less agreement about the extent to which the state, embodied in an elected government, has the right to protect itself against its own citizens by depriving them of information which might make them critical of it, or which, in its judgement, might be morally deleterious to it or to them.

Many of these long-standing issues have been exacerbated and re-emphasized by the information and communications revolution of the late 20th century. The proponents of stricter moral censorship of television, videos and the internet, for example, insist that their easy availability in virtually every home imposes a duty on producers, broadcasting organizations and other information providers to maintain high standards. There is, of course, no common agreement on what these standards should be, nor on a politically and socially acceptable mechanism for enforcing them. Even this debate, however, familiar as it still is, could be argued to be losing its relevance. Satellite broadcasting is extra-territorial; we are years and possibly decades away from international treaties which will impose uniform moral regimes on transnational and international broadcasters. Domestic use of simple technologies (like DVD recorders or satellite television decoders) is almost impossible to control. Film censorship, for example, was viable for so long as movies could only be watched on television or at the cinema; the advent of video made it impossible to enforce except against the shops from which the videos or DVDs are bought or rented. Once they have been obtained, nothing can prevent their private viewing, any more than it is possible to prevent the use of printed pornography once it has evaded any laws which attempt to prevent its distribution. Using the law against networked pornography is also proving to be very difficult, although not impossible. Technology has not won the battle against the censors, but it has redrawn the map of the battlefield and rewritten the rules of engagement. Moral censorship has become largely a matter of personal choice and the efforts of the state are directed towards areas – such as child pornography – where there is virtually universal agreement that the material is unacceptable.

Control of content, however, is only one of the challenges posed to states and their citizens by the use of information and communication technologies. Even in comparatively innocuous matters, like the enforcement of copyright law, the use of the internet is posing unprecedented challenges. The music industry was in danger of being destabilized by the simplicity of downloading, reproduction and performance, and more complex uses such as mixing and re-issuing. The industry responded by developing both technical systems and business models which allowed the distribution and purchase of music online. This seems likely to become the principal channel through which popular music (and an increasing quantity of classical music) will be disseminated in the future. Similar issues are to be found in the publishing industry. The issues surrounding the economics of electronic journals (discussed

briefly in Chapter 3) are far from being addressed by the development of
new business models. Like the music industry, the publishers are
exploiting new technologies when they are able to do so; books on
demand (BOD) is one example, but the development of e-books (or
rather of culturally acceptable reading devices) is likely to be the next
great breakthrough.

These developments do, however, raise some interesting and difficult
issues. A generation is maturing in the industrialized world to whom the
very concept of copyright is fundamentally unconvincing. If the purpose of
the use of internet is to disseminate information and facilitate access to it,
why, it is asked, should there be any limits on the use of content? The
answer, of course, lies in the need to make it economically viable to
generate high-cost information; but the operation of the information
market-place in the future will result in the availability of far more free
goods than has been the case in the age of print.

The balance between producer and consumer of information, and
between the roles of the state and the individual in its creation and
dissemination, is changing. Historically, the state has been a spectator, a
protector and a regulator. Intermittently, it has also been a participant, as
propagandist or monopoly supplier. Now it is, increasingly, a competitor
in the information market-place where it is only one of many powerful
agencies. It seeks to manipulate the market and customers, as well as
being a collector of information and subject to its own rules about the
storage, use and dissemination of the information which it collects. The
balance between the obligation of the state to provide information and its
duty to protect itself by secrecy has been struck in different ways in
different countries. In all states, however, even in the most open
democracies, there is clearly a distinction, however its boundaries are
defined, between the public and private spheres of government
information. But the boundaries are blurring, partly because it is so easy
to put information into the public domain, and partly because there is a
growing expectation that this will happen.

Similarly, there is a distinction, equally difficult to define, between the
state as a provider of factual information and the state as the generator of
propaganda. Promoting its own country is a necessary part of the function

of any government. Many countries have developed institutions and agencies which have a specific responsibility to do so. Some of these agencies are overtly propagandist, while others concentrate on the promotion of educational and cultural links with other countries. In either case, it can be cogently argued that national self-promotion is one of the legitimate functions of government. Domestically, however, this can easily slide into political propaganda whose purpose is partisan rather than general. In totalitarian states, the sole purpose of government information agencies is to disseminate the information (whether true or not) which portrays the government in the best light. Suppression of unwelcome truths, favourable interpretations of events and the invention or falsification of 'facts' are all part of the armoury of the propagandist. Propaganda, in various guises, has been a tool of the state since states first existed, but the evolution and development of sophisticated systems of communication have greatly facilitated its use and increased its effectiveness.

Almost as soon as it was invented, the printing press was adopted for propagandist purposes. It has indeed been forcefully argued that printing was a major factor in the success of the Protestant Reformation. The proposition is, by its nature, neither provable nor refutable, but it is unquestionable that the easy availability of a simple technology for communicating information and opinion over time and distance was a significant difference between the 16th century and earlier periods in which reform of the Church had been attempted. Newspapers were first used as propaganda tools during the Thirty Years War in Germany (1618–48) and the contemporary Civil War in England (1642–9); they have been used in every European war since then, and throughout the world as European technology and influence spread across the globe.

It was, however, the 20th century which saw the triumph of propaganda. Totalitarian states of both the left and the right, and both governments and oppositions in the democracies, exploited the potential of the new mass media. The first medium to be used in this way was the cinema, seen by Lenin as the most important means of bringing 'information' to the people of the newly created Soviet Union. In Germany after 1933, the Nazis exploited films in the same way, both by overt propaganda, as in the newsreels, and by more subtle means. Two of the greatest film-makers of the 1920s and 1930s, Eisenstein in the USSR and Riefenstahl in Germany, for all their undoubted artistic achievements, were propagandists working for the success of political programmes in which they profoundly believed.

Radio also served a propagandist purpose. Hitler, a brilliant orator, exploited it to the full. So did two of his bitterest foes, Churchill and Roosevelt. All were masters of the spoken word. Roosevelt, in particular, developed a radio style, very different from traditional platform oratory, which brought something like domesticity to his promotion of his administration's policies into almost every American home. These examples show how difficult it is to define the concept of propaganda. The term is perhaps too emotive, too suggestive of falsehood and the promotion of the undesirable. What is certain, however, is that the mass media of the early and middle decades of the 20th century gave politicians unprecedented access to those over whom they ruled, and upon whose support and votes some of them depended.

The use of the media by political parties and governments continues to be a political issue in its own right. At the same time, however, there is what is probably generally regarded as a legitimate area of government activity in information provision. Although sometimes the subject of political controversy, it is broadly accepted that such comparatively neutral matters as anonymized or statistical information relating to health, social security benefits, personal safety, crime prevention, and the like are proper subjects for information dissemination by governments. Like other information providers, governments will use whatever seems to be the most efficient and cost-effective means of reaching its target audience. This might be advertisements in newspapers or in the cinema or on television, or leaflets provided through libraries, Citizens Advice Bureaux or even directly to every household. Like advertisers, government agencies have to undertake appropriate market research to determine how they can best get their message to the intended recipients.

This reveals yet again the conflict which is inherent in government involvement in information collection and dissemination. On the one hand, its concern is with secrecy, and, on the other, with dissemination. It has both constraints and requirements imposed on it by the law. The unique capacity of government to collect information at a national level, and to make it available both nationally and internationally, makes it an important operator in the information market-place. Governments are major publishers both of priced and free publications. They own large and complex websites. They are, either directly or indirectly, the principal funders of public, school and university libraries. At the same time, they are the protectors of vast quantities of personal data, and also of information which they regard as being potentially too damaging to the national interest to be made available at all. The intrinsic contradictions in these many and varied roles are obvious, and the potential for conflicts of interest between one part of government and another, and, even more importantly, between governors and governed, are equally clear.

Even governments, however, must make use of channels of communication provided by the private sector, and take account of their influence. The relationship between government and the media in an open society can never be a comfortable one; indeed, it might be argued that it should not be. On the other hand, governments have a regulatory role in ensuring that the media, and the providers of telecommunications systems, work in a way which, while not inhibiting profit, is for the general good. Questions which can be formulated about the role of the state in controlling the flow of information in a free society inevitably lead into even more difficult questions about the role of the media and the providers of telecommunications networks in such a society, some of which go beyond our present concerns.

It is one of the hallmarks of democracy that the press and the broadcasting media are not under the editorial control of government, although the extent of their freedom varies greatly from one country to another. In the USA, for example, there is almost total freedom within broad constitutional and legal constraints relating to libel, security, and the like. In some western European countries, on the other hand, at least until recently, the government exercised substantial control over the output of the state broadcasting organizations in both radio and television; this was the case in both France and Italy. Recent technological developments have fundamentally changed the ability of the state to intervene in the affairs of broadcasters. The internationalization of television through the use of satellite transmission has effectively undermined the power of the state to control what is received, even when reception is theoretically illegal. In practice, power over the content of satellite television rests almost entirely with the owners and employees of the broadcasting organizations. Satellite news services, such as those of CNN and the BBC's World Service Television, have revolutionized the availability of news and comment in many countries whose own broadcasters are under strict state control. In that sense, satellite television has broken the state monopoly control of the network infrastructure, and multichannel television, much of it extra-territorial, has become a major cultural and political force.

Overt control, however, is not the only way in which the state intervenes in broadcasting and other forms of information dissemination. The power exercised by democratic governments includes the power to restrict and to disseminate information. The presentation of this information has been increasingly professionalized. Government spokespersons are paid to put government policies in a favourable light; opposition political parties employ people to do the same, and when they take office continue and develop the practices of their predecessors. In itself, there is nothing 'right' or 'wrong' about this, although there may be a debate about who should pay for the process. What is clear, however, is that access to the broadcast media, and the control of the flow of information and guidance on its interpretation, have become an integral part of the political process in democratic states. In part, this is a response to the ease of access to information which the media now provide. In the UK, for example, there were no 24/7 news broadcasts in 1990; in 2008, a subscriber to BSkyB can access several, including some in languages other than English and many which originate outside the country. There are websites and e-mail-based lists which specialize in circulating information – sometimes true, sometimes not – which governments seek to control. It has become almost impossible for the state to have secrets even in wartime. The response of the state has been to compete in the information market-place; the spin doctors and the embedded journalists are just two aspects of the response.

At the same time, the media corporations have become even more powerful. Even more than governments, these organizations can control and manipulate the flow of information. Where cross-media ownership is permitted, so that the same company can be involved in, for example, television and newspapers, this makes the media giants far more potent than any democratic state has ever aspired to be, and far more potent in practice than all but the most successful of totalitarian states have succeeded in being. Both the press and television exercise great influence by their selection of news and by their presentation of it. Even where 'objectivity' is sought, the very process of selection (which is inevitable) means that it cannot truly be achieved. The role of the journalist, the editor and the media owner thus becomes that of a gatekeeper of information and former of opinion.

There are indeed some developments which go some way towards counterbalancing the potential influence of the transnational mass media. Of these, by far the most important is the world wide web, especially in its latest manifestations as the social web. Organizations, interest groups and individuals have created millions of websites. Tiny groups of people who share a common interest can bring their interest into the public sphere. The web effectively gives every user the power to publish, and to do so in an arena where there are almost no controls over content. The web offers a meaningful opportunity to bypass existing commercial and governmental information and communications systems. As we saw in Chapter 4, the academic networks which have been developed throughout the industrialized world are now linked through the internet to permit virtually uncontrolled, and normally uncharged, access to vast stores of information. The present structure of the internet, which reflects its unplanned origin and growth, allows anyone with network access to search for information of interest, and to contribute to thousands of ongoing debates, use public access databases, and the like. The networks allow individual information -seekers to search directly and personally for their information, and for individual providers to make such information available with virtually no editorial, commercial or political control.

Fears are expressed about whether this freedom can be allowed to continue; doubts have been expressed about whether it should be. Abuse of the system and perhaps fear of its potential will inevitably lead to regulation. A new kind of argument is being deployed in which the control of flows of information is represented as an essential weapon in the 'war' against international terrorism and criminality. Some governments are arguing that further limits on personal freedom are essential to protect the greater good of the community, and that this will include control of the internet. The complex relationship between information, the state and citizen will thus continue to evolve. As it does so, the role of the intermediary will also change, for the ever-growing size and complexity of information sources and systems inevitably means that information-seekers will need help. Some of this comes from within the systems themselves, but there is still a need for gatekeepers and guides who can assist individuals to exploit to the full the vast stores of information which are available to them. It is the role of these functionaries – the information professionals – that we shall consider in Chapter 7.

PART 4
The information profession

Chapter 7

The information profession: a domain delineated

The information needs of governments, institutions, businesses and individuals can be satisfied only if they can be matched to the available resources, and those resources can then be made accessible to the potential users. The quantity and complexity of information, and of the systems and services through which it can be provided, have grown in tandem with the growth of our information needs and our dependence upon effective provision. The information professionals would seem to be the intermediaries between information sources, information systems and information users. They might be – perhaps should be – key players in the information society. In this chapter, we shall explore their role.

If we consider the various issues which have been discussed in the previous chapters of this book, we can identify three strands of information which interlock but which are essentially different. These might be defined as:

- public information
- personal information
- private information.

We shall also need to consider three similarly interwoven aspects of information storage and provision. These are:

- information sources
- information networks and systems

• information agencies.

The distinction between them is critical to understanding the proper role of the information professional.

For our purposes, *public* information is information which is intended to be in the public domain. This statement, however, needs some further refinement. The phrase 'public domain' is not used here as it is used by an intellectual property lawyer; in that context, it means information, texts, designs, and so on which are no longer protected by the relevant laws, and can be freely used, copied and reproduced, like a book whose copyright has expired. In the present context, the phrase is used less precisely, to mean information which is intended to be publicly available within the normal constraints of law and commerce. By this definition, any information on the web is in the public domain even if a charge is made for access. Similarly, the information in any book is also in the public domain. In both cases, of course, the copyright may not be. A website or a book has been created to be circulated (whether without charge, by access charge, by outright purchase or by loan) and then read in whole or in part. There are indeed some factors which might inhibit the unlimited circulation of a book. It has to be bought either by the reader or by someone (such as a librarian) on the reader's behalf. A non-purchaser who seeks to read a book must have access to a library which stocks it, and then find it in stock when it is sought, and so on. These, however, are minor obstacles, and largely inapplicable to websites. For printed documents, they are of some practical importance but do not affect the basic principle that the clear intention of the author and publisher of this or any other book is that it should be available to the public at large.

Public domain information – collected, analysed and prepared for use – takes many forms. A conventionally published printed book is a useful paradigm of the phenomenon, but by no means the only example. Statistical information assembled by governments, for example, is available through electronic media and in various printed publications. Some of it is free of charge; some (such as online access to certain databases or some government publications) is very expensive to obtain. The principle, however, is unaffected: the information is intended for public use, and the monetary cost of obtaining it is no more than a financial transaction designed to offset the costs of providing it and perhaps to generate a surplus which will sustain the business of the providers.

Once this concept of public domain information is accepted, the distinction between it and *private* information is comparatively easy to establish and define. It is simply information which is not intended for public circulation, having been assembled and stored to satisfy some private purpose. Uncontentious examples include marketing information assembled by a company, which would be valuable to its competitors (and probably acquired more cheaply by copying) and whose general availability would therefore be disadvantageous to those who had incurred the expense of collecting it. There is probably no serious disagreement about the legitimacy of the general concept of commercial confidentiality of this kind, and hence of the basic principle of the legitimate existence of information which is not publicly available. Other issues are less straightforward. Governments and their agencies are also involved in this sphere of information, and, as has been suggested in Chapter 6, there are different views of the proper boundaries between the private and public domains, symbolized in the different traditions which have prevailed in the past in the UK and the USA.

The distinction which is being suggested between private and *personal* information is essentially that between information relating to institutions, organizations, companies and groups, on the one hand, and, on the other hand, information relating to identifiable individuals. Again, however, there are few absolutes. While it would be generally agreed that information relating to a person's health, for example, is indeed private and should be confidential, there are circumstances in which it inevitably and properly becomes known to others. In the case of health information, the 'others' include doctors and paramedics who treat the data subject, and, with the data subject's consent, might also include insurance companies or employers. Professional ethical codes are sometimes as important as the law in regulating the use and dissemination of private information. To develop this example further, there may be ethical considerations about informing a patient's family, or even patients themselves, about the diagnosis or prognosis of a particular medical condition.

Moreover, some personal information might, with the data subject's passive consent, be made available to others, usually in a non-attributable form. Information collected for census purposes, for example, or by market research companies, is not published in a form which allows individuals to be identified, even though this identification may be known to the data collector and be stored in the data files. In some circumstances, data subjects may even allow attributable data to be made available; for example, in giving consent for one's name and address to be on a particular mailing list, one may give or refuse consent for that mailing list to be sold to other organizations.

The role of the information professional

We turn now to our second set of factors which underpin our understanding of the functions and responsibilities of the information professional.

Information *sources* are the essential basis upon which all information provision rests. For much of the last 500 years, this has primarily meant printed sources, although orality was never, as we saw in Chapters 1 and 2, entirely lost or forgotten. In the last 150 years, the development of new media for the storage and dissemination of information products has multiplied the variety of sources, and has been a factor in greatly increasing their number. The contents of such sources of information are more readily accessible when they are deliberate creations rather than accidental accumulations. Even if the accretion of information (or information media) is partly random, its effective use requires systematic organization. A library is a useful paradigm here. Even the most systematically assembled library can be used only if its contents are recorded in an equally systematic way, and those records provide access to the books in the library. The catalogue, and perhaps the classification of the books by subject (which may be reflected in their order on the shelves), thus becomes a key tool in the effective exploitation of the library as an information resource.

All information sources, to be effective, need to be similarly systematic in their organization. In books, for example, the table of contents, the index and even such mundane matters as the page numbers, are all part of a design which allows the book to be used. The arrangement of the data is even more important. Even books which consist principally of continuous prose are easier to use if there is an alphabetic index to their subject matter. Some books are actually built around such a list; a dictionary is perhaps the most perfect example, but there are, of course, many other reference books which work on the same principle. In considering the sources of information, therefore, we are looking at their format and their arrangement, as well as at their contents. The same basic principles apply to the design of a database or a website to facilitate access. A well designed website is easy to find and easy to navigate, with appropriate metadata and well developed and logically selected links to and from other pages and sites. Crucially, there must also be a means of finding the information source so that it can be used. For printed products, this is the function of bibliographies, catalogues, abstracts and indexes. For electronic resources, the critical factor is the use of metadata to describe the source, which will enable search engines and web crawlers to discover it and hence to present it to the searcher. The technology (and indeed the retrieval capacity) may be vastly different, but the underlying principles remain essentially the same.

It is the content which is the *raison d'être* of a book or any other information object. If a source is to be used effectively and confidently, there have to be some standards for making a qualitative assessment of it. For all factual information, the minimal requirement is accuracy, so far as that can be attained; to validate that, it is common practice to give a source for the information, or at least some account of other sources from which it can be verified. In the past, this quality control has rested largely with editors and publishers. As we have seen in Chapters 3 and 4, however, traditional methods are breaking down even in the publishing industry, for both economic and technological reasons. On the internet, there are only whatever standards web authors and other information providers apply to themselves, although these do include many examples of formal editorial control in the case of, for example, the content of electronic peer reviewed journals.

Information *networks and systems* are the means by which information is stored and disseminated. The basic concept of the network is that of providing a communications link, regardless of the form which that link might take. We can properly refer to a road network, or a telephone network, as well as an information network or a computer network. Both networks and systems are now usually associated with the use of computers, but the terminology can usefully be extended to other methods of storage and dissemination. In the library world, for example, the word 'network' has long been used to describe a group of libraries which collaborate or interact over some purpose such as interlending or other co-operative activities intended to benefit their clients.

Networks are essential in the provision of information, since no individual provider or agency can be in possession of all the information which might be required by clients. It is only through networks which link providers with one other, and with the sources to which each has access, that clients can be fully and effectively served. This is most easily described as an information *system*. This might indeed be a complex computer-based system, but it might be very simple local agreements about library co-operation or informal personal contacts. In essence, however, information systems have a common purpose: to anticipate demand for information so that such a demand can, through their operation, be effectively met.

There is no intrinsic reason why information provision should be institutionalized, but, in practice, it has normally been delivered through an *agency*. Again, a word is being used here with a very wide and general application. The agency may be an individual (more properly called an *agent*) or it may be an organization or institution. It may be part of a larger body, like the information section in a business, or it may be a distinctive body in its own right, like a national library. Perhaps most agencies, like the libraries of universities, fall somewhere in between. The precise distinctions do not concern us. The important point is that an information agency (or agent) provides a point of contact between the information-seeker and the information which is contained in and derived from various sources and then delivered through networks and systems to the end-user.

It is this aspect of access to information that has been changed most significantly in the last decade. We might compare the world wide web to a universal library; indeed, this was how Nelson conceptualized the application of hypertext. There are, however, fundamental differences. The most obvious is the sheer size and scale of the web compared with even the largest physical libraries. This, however, is the least important distinction. A library consists of a body of information media which has been through at least one, and often several, selection processes. At the very least it has been selected for the library; in practice almost everything in a library will have been selected and edited by a publisher, perhaps making use of expert or specialist advice during the process. That is simply not true of the web. Author and publisher can be (and often are) the same. Quality control is entirely in the hands of the provider. There has been an important shift in the balance of power between the author and the publisher; the latter has been effectively eliminated from web-based dissemination of information. But there has also been a shift in the balance of responsibility between provider (whether author or publisher or both) and consumer. The information user cannot assume that there has been any verification or quality control of content on the web, and must bring a different level of critical faculty to its use.

In bringing together the concepts of public, private and personal information on the one hand, and information sources, information networks and systems, and information agencies, on the other, we can begin to define the concept of the *information professional*. At each stage in the processes that have been described both in the first few pages of this chapter and in the earlier chapters of this book, we can identify some familiar occupational groups who are involved in them. These most obviously include publishers, librarians and archivists, but there are many others. The authors and compilers of information sources clearly play an important role, and they must be added to our list. The managers of information networks and systems provide the essential infrastructure for information delivery to end-users; some such managers call themselves 'librarians' but many more do not. The title may be as vague as 'information officer' or as apparently precise as 'system manager'. Do all of these groups constitute a single profession? If they do, what are its characteristics, and what is its role in an increasingly information-dependent society? And what, if any, is the role of that profession in the open domain of the internet and the world wide web? Do we need professionals when everyone with internet access can search for information for themselves?

The work of the information professional

Some of these questions can more easily be answered if we consider a few exemplary cases of those who work with information. In Chapter 3, we looked at aspects of the work of the authors and publishers of books, and at the means of book production, distribution and sale. In the simplest case of a book written by one person, that person – the author – is the originator, analyst and guarantor of the information which the book contains. Authors may seek to bolster their own authority by relying on that of others; this is the purpose of citations of sources and similar devices. The substantive intellectual input of the author is in the interpretation, selection and presentation of the material, much of which may already, as a collection of related but separate facts, be familiar to many of the book's readers. The publisher's role is quite different. The publishing function is essentially that of facilitation, making possible the production and distribution of the author's work by providing both the capital investment and technical skills that are needed to enable it to reach its intended market and audience. Where are the information skills in this process?

If we see the writing, publishing and sale of books as part of a continuous chain of communication of information from author to reader, then we can cogently argue that both author and publisher are indeed professionally involved with information. In neither case, however, is this to be understood as meaning that they necessarily possess or need specific professional qualifications or training. The publisher may indeed do so, although in British publishing this is still comparatively uncommon, but the author almost certainly will not. Both require, no doubt, a good general education and high levels of literacy and its associated skills, but these are not acquired through the sort of formal processes of examination and monitoring of practice which we associate with professions such as law or medicine. Perhaps it would be more terminologically accurate to say that authors and publishers are occupationally involved with information, although, for reasons which will be suggested later, the very word 'professional' is becoming less exclusive and defining than it used to be.

When we move away from the simple model of the single-authored book, however, we have to consider different factors. Even in a comparatively straightforward case, such as a volume of essays by several writers with an editor, the role of the editor is not only intellectually different from that of an author working alone but also involves other skills. The editor will, for example, be expected to impose a uniformity of technical style on the contributors. This is not an aesthetic matter of prose style as it might be understood by a literary critic, but style in the narrower technical sense, such as forms of bibliographical references, and the almost invisible issues of uniformity of spellings where there are alternatives (-ise/-ize endings, for example), hierarchies of headings and subheadings, and the use of typographical devices such as bold and italic. These issues, which fundamentally effect the readability and hence the utility of the book, are essentially professional. They may be undertaken by an employee or agent of the publisher, or by the editor of the volume, acting *de facto* in that capacity. Whoever is responsible, that person is making information more accessible to the user, and functioning, in part, as an information professional.

If we consider the case of the compiler and editor of a reference book or (analogously for this purpose) a database, these issues are further clarified. A reference tool, whether it is on paper or in electronic form, is only as efficient as its design. Basic decisions about the order and form of entries, and the means of accessing the information through indexes and other devices, will determine how well, and perhaps even whether, it can be used. Few reference books, and almost no public databases, are compiled by a single individual. Therefore, rules are needed which systematically regulate the entries and can be unambiguously applied by all the contributors, perhaps over many years. To the librarian, a cataloguing code is the most obvious and familiar example of such a set of rules. Without such a code, a catalogue makes no sense. When such a code is properly written and uniformly applied, however, the standardization and compatibility of catalogues are assured. During the last 25 years, the *Anglo-American Cataloguing Rules* in their second edition

(AACR2) have been adopted throughout the world as a standard code. Closely related to them have been other forms of bibliographical standardization like the MARC format for machine-readable catalogues, and the International Standard Book Description (ISBD). As a result, it has been possible to create compatible catalogues in different institutions. Libraries have been able to share the costs of cataloguing and to 'buy' their catalogue records from a central source such as a national bibliographical agency or a book supplier. Costs have been cut, standards raised and access simplified. All of this has been achieved through imposing uniform standards on electronic databases. We now express this in terms of metadata (as a form of cataloguing) and ontology (the classification of knowledge) but the essential principles remain unchanged.

On a smaller scale, the same principle applies to any multi-authored work of reference. A dictionary or encyclopedia has an internal logic and arrangement to which all contributors are expected to adhere, and which the editors will impose on the contributions of those who deviate from it. In a dictionary, for example, editorial policy will determine whether each word is defined, whether an etymology is given, whether there are examples of usage, and so on. The same principle applies to all reference works of this kind. It also applies, and perhaps even more strictly, to a database. The obvious advantages of an electronic database over a printed source – currency and ease of access – can be achieved only if the database design is appropriate. This means that before a single entry is compiled and entered, the designer must try to anticipate both the needs and the expertise of the user. There must also be quality control mechanisms to ensure that each entry complies exactly with the rules which have been determined. When such systems have been devised and implemented, however, there is no limit to the number of contributors who can augment the database, nor, given appropriate network access, any limitation on their locations.

When we consider the compilation of bibliographies, catalogues and reference books, and the design of public access databases, we can perhaps no longer so clearly define the boundaries of professional information work. The editors and the publishers are engaged in a joint enterprise to which each bring their own expertise, but these areas of expertise necessarily overlap. The closeness with which they must work together, often over a long period of time, is quite different from the classical model of the author-publisher relationship.

These examples suggest that the concept of the 'publisher' as an information professional needs to be extended beyond the traditional understanding of the publisher's role. Indeed, the boundaries between publishing and the other functions of information compilation, production and distribution, are, as we have seen in Chapter 3, blurring and perhaps dissolving. When an author 'writes' a book onto a disk, and the file which is created eventually drives the phototypesetter which produces the printing plate, the traditional functions of author, publisher's editor, copy editor and compositor have all changed; that of the compositor may even have been eliminated. The disaggregation and recombination of skills in this model is typical of the changes being wrought by the use of computers in the information world; traditional boundaries are being eroded and there is convergence between traditionally separate activities.

Librarians and libraries: archetypes in transition

In considering some aspects of the work of the librarian, this process is perhaps even more obvious. In some ways, librarians are the archetypal information professionals. Indeed, the terms are often used synonymously, with perhaps a suggestion that the 'information professional' is more modern and forward-looking than the traditional (an epithet increasingly attached) 'librarian'. No such synonymy is being suggested here, but 'librarianship', as it is normally understood and practised, is certainly intended to be encompassed by the broader concept. Historically, the librarian has been the collector and curator of books, making arrangements for them to be inventoried, stored and used, by means of such devices and mechanisms as catalogues, classification schemes, circulation systems, and the like. Inevitably, this has also made librarians the managers of the institutions in which these activities take place, and therefore managers of financial, human and physical resources.

In the last 30 years, however, the role of the librarian has been subject to great change. To some extent this has been a change of emphasis. There is an explicit recognition that it is the provision of information to users which is the driving force of the librarian's work, and that for most users the source of either is a matter of indifference. Quality of service is measured by speed and accuracy of fulfilment of users' demands, not by the number of books in stock or even cruder statistical data such as the number of loans. Even so, the custodial role has not been forgotten, and has not become irrelevant. Information sources have a physical existence, even if it is on a disk in a computer at a site many thousands of miles away from the point of consultation. The information can be accessed only if the medium is sufficiently stable for it to survive. Nevertheless, the custodianship implied by the preservation of such a source is a means to an end, rather than an end itself.

The change of attitude, embodied in the explicit recognition of the primacy of the user rather than the source, was under way long before information technology made its major impact on librarianship from the mid-1970s onwards. Since that time, change has been rapid and profound. The most fundamental tool of the librarian - the catalogue - has been transformed beyond recognition. The online public access catalogue (OPAC) - in effect a bibliographic database of the library's holdings - offers a vast range of services which were never previously available to users. Freed from the physical restraints of the traditional card catalogue, which at its best (rarely attained) normally offered access only by author, subject and title, the user can now search for holdings in a way which meets individual needs rather than the convenience of the managers of the catalogue. This, however, is only the beginning.

Other computer-based tools have wrought a similar revolution in access to information itself. Databases, whether accessed online on distant hosts or locally or through a network on CD-ROM, have supplanted, as has already been suggested, many reference sources which have formerly been available only in print. This fact alone has changed both the technicalities and economics of information provision. Effective use of a database requires some training; it is difficult to use it without some instruction, and almost impossible to use it well. The instruction may be no more than a printed sheet accompanying a CD-ROM – the equivalent of the preface to a reference book – but such instruction (unlike reading a preface) is essential rather than desirable. Technology gives access to vast quantities of information, and yet has made access somewhat more difficult.

Far from eliminating the librarian, the use of technology as the basis of information service provision in institutions and agencies has highlighted the need for people with special skills who can help information-seekers. Nevertheless, the role of those people has changed. In academic libraries, in particular, librarians are increasingly working as the trainers and guides of a computer-literate generation of students who need to be taught the specifics of information searching and retrieval in their own disciplines. In effect, librarians are passing on to their users some of what were traditionally regarded as their own unique professional skills. Despite the inevitable and desirable survival of some mediated searches, in which librarians work on behalf of users, librarians increasingly provide skill-training as well as information. As in the publishing of books, we can see a technology-driven change in the relationship between provider and client, and between the various participants in the chain of information supply and demand.

Library users are becoming much more conscious of these changes and are seeking to exploit them. In libraries in every sector, users are aware of the power of technology to assist in the delivery of services and information. In universities, it is normal for the library catalogue to be mounted on a network which allows academics to access the OPAC from workstations on their own desks. It is sometimes possible to access certain databases or electronic journals in the same way, although where charges are involved (as they often are) this raises administrative issues which need to be addressed, and some uses of databases also raise legal questions about the copyright in the information which is retrieved and about the site licences which allow network access. These administrative issues, however, cannot conceal the fact that the library is no longer defined simply as a location. It has become a concept. The development of the world wide web significantly emphasized this trend. The web can be browsed from any networked computer, using search engines which are designed for the non-expert user. This is a profound shift away from the mediated, library-based search.

As the use of computers becomes more fully integrated in the processes of teaching and learning at all levels, as well as in research, the perception of the library as a room or a building will continue to be challenged by this broader concept of information services provided through various parts of the infrastructure of a school, university or other organization. This does not mean that libraries will vanish. There will still be a need for a bookstore and a place for individual and group-based study. In many cases, the library will also continue to be the most convenient location for the organization's information specialists who help employees, students and the general public to meet their information needs, even if many of the requests and replies are transmitted electronically rather than in person.

Yet even the bookstore element of the library is under threat. All libraries have long since recognized the futility of seeking universal coverage in their own holdings of stock. For much of the 20th century, libraries in Europe and North America were developing relationships with one other which allowed them and their users to share in their respective resources. The most familiar form of such co-operation is the use of interlibrary lending, well established in the developed world for more than half a century. Different models of interlending networks have developed according to local political and financial circumstances, but the basic principle of sharing is common to all of them. Again, however, technology is enabling fundamental changes to be made in the delivery of the service. Traditionally, interlending has involved the physical movement of the desired document from the lender to the borrower. Often, the document was actually a photocopy of a journal article, to be retained by the recipient, but if originals were involved there was also a return movement. The system worked, and often worked well, yet it was both costly and time-consuming. The traditional movement of documents through interlending systems is gradually being replaced by electronic document delivery, using networks to deliver digitized data to the end-user. As the technology of digitization by scanning continues to improve, such systems will become more common.

This raises a host of complex issues which extend far beyond the traditionally perceived boundaries of librarianship. Electronic document delivery is only possible with the consent of the owners of the copyright in the original document, a restriction which does not apply to interlending, except, in a limited way, to the supply of photocopies. If we develop the scenario a little further, we have an electronic journal, available through a centralized electronic document delivery system, in which the 'library' which holds the database containing the journal is actually the 'publisher' of the journal. By this point, such words as 'library' and 'publisher' have developed so far beyond their normal meanings as to have lost them, and the boundaries between the two have all but vanished. In the academic world, this could prove to be the most important convergence of all. As we suggested in Chapter 4, the traditional learned journal is imperilled by the cost of production and distribution; the electronic equivalents, some of which already exist, may be the only viable way forward. If that is indeed the case, it is quite possible that the library's role is moving even further from that of passive provider towards that of active participant in the process of scholarly communication. In the academic world, convergence is developing rapidly. The growth of institutional and subject repositories is a prime example of the trend. An institutional repository – in which all members of the staff of a university are requested (or indeed required) to provide their publications in electronic formats – is now a common feature of almost all research-active universities. It gives the institution, and individuals, a higher profile, probably increases their all-important citation count, and provides a useful shop-window for the scholarly and scientific achievements of the university. By hosting these deposit copies of scholarly publications – with the consent of the publisher – the library is becoming a *de facto* publisher. At discipline level, similar developments are taking place. Subjects as diverse as physics and archaeology have developed large electronic repositories of both publications and datasets which are made generally accessible; indeed in some subjects, those who provide the funds for research typically require that the products are deposited in repositories of this kind. Both institutional and subject repositories (the latter sometimes referred to as data archives) blur the boundaries of the formerly separate: published and unpublished, library and publisher, author and editor. We must, however, be wary of overestimating the rapidity or universality of change and of assuming that it will bring universal benefits. The custodian of books and the provider of information continue to coexist, and may do so for decades to come. The mere existence of libraries, and the vast capital investment which they represent, is perhaps the most important guarantee of their future. Although there are technologies which would make it possible to digitize the world's printed books, the money to facilitate that conversion is not, and will probably never be, available. Moreover, there will be users whose needs will continue to be met most effectively, and perhaps some which can only be met, through the provision of books and documents. The majority of users of British public libraries, for example, are those borrowing books for leisure reading. For so long as that continues to be true, public libraries (which are, after all, supported by the taxes paid by their users) will have to continue to provide access to suitable book stocks. Even in academic libraries, where the demand for sophisticated information provision is great, scholars in many disciplines will continue to read and to publish in traditional formats because there is no practical economic alternative.

The use of new media and information technology can actually make access to information more difficult for less advantaged users, as we have suggested. It was argued in Chapter 5 that the gap between the information rich and information poor is widening as a consequence of the use of computer-based systems for information storage and the gradual elimination of traditional media for some kinds of information source and information retrieval tools. The obstacles for the information poor are many: lack of skills, equipment and the capital investment needed to provide both are only three of the most obvious. Even those with skills and access, however, can encounter serious problems. The very quantity of information which is now theoretically accessible is, paradoxically, making access to any specific piece of information more difficult. The web itself, one of the most potent symbols and powerful products of the information revolution, gives access to so much data that it may be doubted whether any search can realistically expect to find all the relevant information which is available through it. Indeed, the virtually unlimited capacity of users to input data which can be accessed through the internet as a whole emphasizes how important it is for quality control mechanisms, analogous to those in traditional scholarly publishing, to be retained for those electronic communication media which may seek to emulate their

traditionally published predecessors and rivals. The same considerations –
the need for selectivity and for quality control – reiterate the need for
information intermediaries whose skills and expertise become part of the
evaluative process in transmitting information from source to user. The
change is that this role is performed when the information is generated and
stored, not when it is delivered to the end-user.

The use of information technology has nevertheless transformed both
the library and task of the librarian, but it has done so by expansion
rather than by constraint. The skills of information storage, organization,
analysis and retrieval associated with librarians are now in such
widespread demand that they can no longer be regarded as being
uniquely associated with that single profession. At the same time,
however, librarians have learned – and indeed developed – many new
techniques and new skills to meet the changing demands of users and
technology alike. There will be further challenges. The library has become
merely a part of a much larger group of institutions and systems through
which information can be sought and found. Although there may be
qualitative issues about much of the information to be found on the web
and through other internet interfaces, it remains the case that much of it
is reliable and of high quality. Moreover it is easily accessible, and the
rapid development of mobile access devices will only serve to promote the
continued growth in its use. Similarly, the trend towards electronic
publication – for which access across an electronic network is the norm –
will continue to evolve. Electronic journals are only the beginning.
Electronic versions of newspapers are now widely available and heavily
used; e-books are technically (if not yet economically) viable. The 'web
generation' – those born since about 1990 who cannot remember the
world before the web – are now moving into higher education and are
taking into their adult lives fundamentally different expectations about
how they will access and disseminate information, and how they will
communicate both professionally and personally.

These developments have vital implications for librarians. Even the
information management skills which many of them would regard as the
definition of their professional identity are becoming more widespread
among those who were formerly comparatively passive consumers of the

services which librarians provided. At the same time, some of the traditional skills are being displaced without alternatives being developed. The professional staff of a library – to look no further than that well defined and 'traditional' group – increasingly find themselves dealing with the management of the institution and its systems rather than information itself. Users need advice and assistance, but much of it is at a level that can be provided by staff without traditional professional skills and qualifications. There is a growing recognition that there exists a continuum of skills between which there is a gradation rather than sharp dividing lines, and that many information workers in the very near future will be moving through that continuum rather than joining it at a fixed point (such as gaining a particular qualification) and essentially staying there. At the same time, the library itself is being deinstitutionalized. Once we begin to think of a library as a concept rather than a physical entity, it is possible to envisage an information service which is only partly dependent on the existence of a special location in which the functions of storage and use are combined. Some libraries will, for reasons of which some have been suggested here, continue to exist for the foreseeable future, just as the printed document will continue to be the most common single medium for information transfer and storage. Nevertheless, electronic or virtual 'libraries', in which information is provided by network access rather than physical contact with the information source itself, already exist. They are the subject of much further research and development work in several countries. In such a system the role of the information professional is very different from that of the familiar academic librarian. The essential function will be to devise and control systems and to manage information resources so that they are available to all legitimate network users. Professional skills are still needed, and they have something in common, at least conceptually, with the skills of the 'traditional' librarian, but those skills grow out of expertise which is based on an understanding of the management of information and information systems as well as the management of institutions and interpersonal transactions with information-seekers. Indeed, it might be argued that information professionals will be able to move back to their central professional concern with information, information systems and information media if they no longer have to manage complex institutional libraries.

Such a scenario is not the universal future for libraries and librarians. Indeed, the future is likely to be more diverse, and arguably more fragmented, than the past. Institutional libraries, in both the public sphere and in the educational world, will certainly continue to exist both as places of study and as bookstores. They will continue to provide selected materials designed to support the educational requirements and information needs, and perhaps some of the recreational demands, of their various user groups. In particular, the public library system, and the librarians who provide its services, are being pulled in different directions. Public libraries have historically seen their mission as being a ubiquitous provider of information and media. But the recreational role of the public library is beginning to look more comfortable in association with the public provision of leisure and cultural facilities, and perhaps in some cases with the heritage sector. At the same time, however, much teaching and learning will be delivered in ways that are dependent on computer networks; there is a clear and distinctive role for public libraries in supporting education and training at every level. The public library as an information bureau, its third historic role, has also undergone profound change. Here it is closer to the special and academic library sectors, which are themselves becoming less easy to distinguish in the provision of specialist services to business, industry and research and development activities. Economic factors will force the producers and consumers of some information – such as that in scientific journals – to accept new means of access which will, in effect, circumvent the library building, while still needing some of the professional information skills which formerly made the library work. These parallel developments are neither conflicting nor incompatible. For the librarian, the challenge is to be sufficiently flexible in attitude and skills to be able to provide both. The rapid and spontaneous development of information and advice services for the general public outside rather than through existing public library systems suggests that such flexibility may not have been as widespread as might have been desirable in the recent past.

From archivist to records manager

In this context, it is perhaps instructive to look at another manifestation of the information profession in the work of the archivists. Their professional skills have been challenged even more than those of librarians by the development and use of information technology. Despite apparent parallels, and some genuine similarities, librarians and archivists have always done essentially different things. The central concern of archivists is the permanent preservation of the documents in their care, but this has only been achieved at the expense of universality of coverage. Archivists are ruthless in their selection of material for preservation, to the extent that as much as 90% of the documentation created by government departments, private companies and other organizations may be deliberately destroyed so that the remaining material of long-term historical interest can be preserved, organized and made available to users.

Computers have an important role in these traditional processes. Archivists, like librarians, have automated their catalogues and inventories, although perhaps not on so large a scale because of the sheer quantity of retrospective conversion that would be needed. The real impact, however, has been in the fact that computers are now both the generators and the storage systems of vast quantities of information which has traditionally been collected and preserved on paper. One obvious example is census returns. Experiments in the use of computers for storing and processing the statistical data generated by population censuses were first undertaken in the 1950s. Since the 1960s, computers have regularly been used for this purpose. The problem for the archivist is that in order to preserve the data it is also necessary either to preserve the hardware through which the data is accessible or to ensure that data are copied into new formats. This remains a constant problem as systems are now normally replaced in a time-frame shorter than the intervals between the censuses themselves. Archivists were thus forced to address issues raised by electronic information systems as soon as those systems began to be used in activities which traditionally generated archival documents.

Partly because of the very different issues raised by electronic archives, not least in terms of the quantity of data generated (quite apart from the preservation of both information and media), a new and largely separate branch of the profession emerged, which came to be known as records management. The role of records managers is only partly archival. Their primary concern is to ensure that the documentation generated by an organization (whether on paper or in digitized form) is organized and stored in a retrievable way. Much of this data is ephemeral, and may be destroyed within months, or even days, of its creation. Some is of more permanent value, and some, such as employee records, or financial accounts, has to be preserved for legal reasons. One of the tasks of the records manager is to ensure that the various criteria for destruction and preservation are defined and met in line with the organization's obligations and wishes.

With the growth in the use of computers to meet the information needs of organizations, the role of the records manager has become more complex and more important. It is closely related to that of the systems manager, and sometimes more closely resembles the work of the manager of a management information system than that of an archivist. The records manager needs many of the skills of selection and preservation traditionally associated with the archivist, but again we can see the breaking down of traditional boundaries and the increasing difficulties of developing precise definitions of the work of information professionals and the distinctions between them. The records manager, unlike the publisher, the librarian or the archivist, generally operates on the boundaries between the public and private spheres, and perhaps more often in the latter. Publishers, librarians and archivists are all, for the most part, concerned with information which is intended for wide dissemination and public access. The records manager, like some other information professionals, is principally concerned with information collected by an organization for its own purposes and whose availability and circulation is strictly controlled. Generically, this may be described as management information, that is, information that will influence decision-making. While the decisions may be made public, the information which underlies them, at least in its raw form, generally is not.

The private information collected by governments and their agencies, and by companies, is often of immense value. This is perhaps most obviously true where it has a direct commercial relevance. Companies collect information about their markets and their rivals. Much of this may be derived from sources which are in the public domain, but its collection, processing and analysis is a long and expensive process. The value which is added by the process – to an understanding of a commercial rival's market share, for example – is the result of an investment which there is a legitimate need to protect. The management of this information, and of the systems in which it is housed, uses many of the techniques of public information work in libraries and archives, but is fundamentally different in philosophy.

Information managers

Information managers who are running management information systems, decision support systems and similar operations, whether in the public or the private sector, are essentially working for their own organizations, not providing a service to outside clients. Traditionally, these managers have not seen themselves as part of the same profession as librarians and archivists, and have only rarely come from the same educational background or training procedures. Technology, however, is creating a commonality of approach, which is probably leading to a convergence even across what has traditionally been a strongly marked boundary. It is certainly the case that in some companies the distinctions are vanishing. Where once there was a clear difference between the provision of technical information to support research and development activities (in a library), marketing information to support sales (within the sales department) and administrative information to support the management infrastructure, all three are increasingly seen as different aspects of the same task: the provision of effective information to those who need it. The organization of the personnel through whom it is provided has become more fluid as it is recognized that many of the techniques and much of the expensive technology are common to all three strands of information management within the organization.

In Britain, these developments have perhaps been most widely publicized in the healthcare sector. The long-established system of universal public provision supported by taxation was fundamentally changed in the 1980s and early 1990s for political reasons. Those changes highlighted the need for more effective information management at all levels. The underlying philosophy of the changes in healthcare provision was to force providers to operate in a 'market' in which they buy and sell services to one other's patients. The general practitioner with a patient who needed a particular surgical procedure was to 'buy' the operation from a hospital which had the capacity to deliver it, at a price agreed between them. Although the money used for these transactions was still derived ultimately from taxation, its use was intended partly to simulate the private sector.

To support the market orientation of the reorganized health service, a vast information infrastructure was created. In the early years, many serious errors were made, largely through ignorance, and there were some highly publicized cases of hugely expensive and ultimately useless computer systems being bought or developed by those with insufficient expertise to manage the projects for which they were responsible. There has, however, been a gradual recognition of the need to develop information management expertise in the sector, or to import it from outside. An infrastructure of training and skill development gradually evolved in the early 1990s. Information management became the linchpin upon which the whole system depended. In the general practitioner's surgery, patient records were automated. Classification systems were developed which allowed diseases and conditions on the one hand, and treatments on the other, to be encoded, and perhaps ultimately matched through the use of expert systems or decision support systems. Hospitals managed their waiting lists, and matched patient needs with the availability of facilities and expertise, in even more complex systems. The management of the whole system of 'payments' largely depended on the effective operation of systems that record the transactions which have taken place. A sector that once employed a few score librarians as its only information professionals became irrevocably committed to the use of information professionals at the core of the management of its activities. It became the archetype of the management of information in the private domain. The essential elements of the information systems that were developed survived successive administrative reorganizations of the service; they also absorbed substantial resources and became an important dimension of the debates about the funding of public provision of healthcare.

The management of health information, however, also impinges, through the records of individual patients, on the most difficult area of all, that of personal information. In a technical sense, there is no distinction that can usefully be made between how different kinds of information are stored. A public document (such as a library catalogue), a private record (such as the transactions between a medical practice and a hospital) and personal data (such as a bank account) all use the same technology, and apply it in much the same way in the creation and maintenance of carefully designed and structured databases which allow the information to be retrieved in the desired format. The differences lie in access rather than storage. As we have seen in Chapter 6, the law regulates many important aspects of this, especially in the control of access to (and to a lesser extent accuracy of) private information about identifiable individuals. Beyond the law, however, there are broadly recognized ethical requirements on information professionals about the use that they make of information that they obtain in performing their duties. Professional bodies have tried, with some success, to define these ethical constraints, although perhaps with more success in the traditional fields such as librarianship and archive work than in the new work sectors for information professionals that are appearing across the whole spectrum of government, industry and public services.

The adoption of computers as the universal tool of information storage and retrieval has made it difficult and perhaps futile to attempt to put a fence around the information professions. As the computer revolution continues, more and more work will be concerned with information handling, even in the manufacturing and production sectors where the processes involved are themselves increasingly automated and computer controlled and thus information dependent. Computers have made explicit what has always been implicit but hidden, ignored and perhaps even unrecognized: that all work which involves making decisions also involves the use of information. Without information, decisions are merely guesses. As information supply becomes more efficient, more accurate and more accessible, the basis for decision-making improves. Ultimately, the quality of the decision will still depend on the interpretative skills of the decision-maker, but the information provider can at least try to ensure that those skills are deployed to the best advantage on the basis of comprehensive knowledge.

In that sense, all 'professional' work, and much that would not be traditionally identified as being 'professional' at all, is information work. In practice, however, decision-makers are dependent on a flow of information that comes to them through intermediaries. These intermediaries may be colleagues, whether as managers, or subordinates or people from outside their own organizations. Ultimately, however, the information that they provide – if it is to be accurate and useful – is drawn from verifiable and reliable sources, accessible to them, from which they can derive what they need and then package it in a form appropriate for the end-user. This intermediary role is that of the information professional, whatever the job title of the person undertaking it.

Managing knowledge

In this book, we have carefully avoided extended discussions of some of the underlying theoretical issues about the nature and concept of information. The approach has been pragmatic and empirical, in the belief that this offers a means of gaining a basic understanding of the social, political, professional and ethical issues which are being generated by our growing dependence on computer networks in almost every aspect of our lives. The same approach is valuable in considering the currently fashionable concept of 'knowledge management'. Information scientists have always, in general terms, taken the view that information is comprised of data and that selected, analysed and processed information constitutes knowledge. As a working definition, this serves us well. In some respects, however, it is not wholly adequate.

Most of the practices and systems which we have discussed in this book have been concerned with what we might call formal information and knowledge. This phrase conveniently describes data which have been brought together in a systematic way. The collected data are, in effect, transformed into information through a systematic analysis and presentation. This may take the form of a book, a website or a database. Through the use and analysis of information, knowledge is acquired; in a research process, new knowledge is generated. It is clearly the case, however, that not all knowledge is acquired in this way. Elaborate taxonomies have been developed to describe the various categories of knowledge, to take account of such phenomena as instinctive or genetically inherited knowledge, or knowledge acquired by experience rather than by formal learning. Knowledge management is an attempt to grapple with the capture, analysis, storage and effective retrieval of informally acquired knowledge.

The problem is particularly acute in organizations. However professionally an organization is managed and operated, the thousands of separate processes involved in providing a service or making a product are ultimately dependent upon the people who undertake them. The more complex the tasks that are undertaken by individuals, the more likely it is that they evolve their own strategies for meeting organizational objectives. Their success is measured by their output rather than by their methods. A key aspect of knowledge management is an attempt to capture for the benefit of the organization the informal knowledge that underpins its effective operation. The importance of this cannot be overestimated at a time when there is a buoyant labour market and rapid movement between jobs by many professionals. How different this really is from information management in the broader sense is perhaps open to question, but it is certainly the case that the effective management of both formal and informal information is the marker, and perhaps the definition, of the information society.

The response of the information professions to the changes taking place all around them has not always been either rapid or effective. Perhaps a profession – especially one like librarianship, which has had a long struggle for public acceptance – is inherently conservative. Of course, there have been individuals, and indeed whole sectors of library service provision, where profound change has been welcomed and well managed. It might be argued, however, that the information profession *as a whole* has come dangerously close to missing an historically unique opportunity to claim a newly developing territory for its own. The skills of information organization and management, combined with the interpersonal skills of service provision and the managerial skills of organizational leadership, are uniquely combined in the information profession. Yet there is ample evidence of a lack of imagination – and perhaps a lack of the necessary political skills - to promote the contribution that information professionals can make to the social, economic and cultural change which is directly or indirectly affecting the lives of every man, woman and child on the planet.

Afterword:
an information society?

It may seem strange at this stage to put a question mark at the end of the title of this last section. There is, however, a real question to be answered. Throughout this book, there has been an emphasis on fundamental continuities as well as profound change. The step from cuneiform to computer was a huge one, encompassing almost the whole consciously recorded history of mankind, and yet in another sense it was not so great. Our remote ancestors who recorded their activities and tried to control their systems of government were responding to the same instincts and imperatives that still drive us today. We have developed previously unimaginable technologies, and new techniques to accompany them, and perhaps we are more systematic in our approach to our use of them, but is the change really more significant than the continuity? If ours is an 'information society', was not the same true of ancient Babylon?

Implicit in the use of the phrase is the suggestion that the information society is a product of the use of computers and other electronic and audiovisual media. In this narrower sense, change has clearly been fundamental. Devices that are now part of our everyday lives – telephones, televisions, computers – were invented within the last 100 years or so and have clearly transformed the way we live and work. That transformation took place within a timescale as short as a decade in many aspects of office management, telecommunications and some forms of television broadcasting. It will continue, for there is every reason to suppose that the pace of change in the immediate future will be as fast as it has been in the immediate past. Indeed, experience and historical precedent would suggest that the pace will, if anything, increase.

Much of this book has been concerned with the consequences of these changes. We have traced the development and impact of a market-place in which information and the media that carry it are commodities to be traded between suppliers and consumers. We have considered some of the social and political issues that have arisen out of the existence of the market-place and the demand for information that created and sustains it. Some of these issues are new, but many are old, although they have been redefined as a consequence of technological innovation. The ownership of information has been a matter of discussion since the 16th century, and regulated by the law for nearly 300 years. Access to information has been a matter of concern to both governments and governed for at least as long. The cost of information, and of the provision of services through which it can be accessed, are both questions with a long ancestry. Yet the way in which these questions are now formulated, and the urgency with which they need to be answered, is indeed different. It is that difference which has a technological origin.

The computer has already been responsible for the most important change in human communications since the invention of printing, and, arguably, since the invention of writing itself. Indeed, printing was merely a development of writing, a technology which enabled writing to become more widespread and the written word to be more uniform and perhaps more reliable. Computing offers far more than that, because it gives the facility, which printing and writing never gave, for instantaneous communication on many different levels. Through the interlinking of computers and telecommunications systems – information technology – individuals can communicate with one other, can access vast stores of information, and can store information for themselves. The form, time and place of output can be largely determined by the convenience of the user rather than that of the provider. At the basis of this lies a common technology, which, while it is vastly complicated, has become so simple that all but a handful of its users can actually ignore its complications. Using a computer has become as much a part of life in the 21st century as switching on an electric light or driving a car.

It is in this ease and universality of access that there lies the key to the information technology revolution and the society that is developing around it. We have indeed always been dependent upon information, but we are now also dependent upon a technology that stores that information for us. In a sense that was always true, but the computer is much more than a passive store like a book or a library. When appropriately instructed, a computer can process and analyse information, and communicate it to other computers. It is this capacity for interactivity with other computers which puts their users in a uniquely powerful position, and differentiates computers themselves fundamentally from all previous mechanisms for the storage and retrieval of information. The combination of the virtually unlimited storage capacity of the computer with a processing power that is also, for all practical purposes, unlimited, makes it a unique and unprecedentedly powerful and potentially dangerous tool. If we are, as a society, concerned about such issues as data protection, it is because we are conscious of the ease with which information can be stored, sorted and retrieved. If we are concerned about the viability of our systems of scholarly communications, it is because we can see the potential of information technology to displace those that we have with something so different, perhaps so much more powerful, that we both fear it and welcome it.

In this narrower sense, the information society can perhaps best be understood as a society that has developed information technology and is learning how to use it. We are at a very early stage in this process. The computer itself is little more than 50 years old even in its most primitive form. In its familiar form, as a desktop microcomputer, it has been with us for less than 30 years. The communications networks that now link millions of such machines across the globe are less than half that age. New devices and new applications are being developed every day. It is, however, clear that the change is irreversible. Nothing will ever be the same again. Like nuclear energy, the power of the computer will have to be controlled if it is to work for our benefit, and we have not yet fully absorbed all its implications for the relationships between individuals, the states of which they are citizens, and indeed between states themselves. At one level, the computer is an empowering tool, which gives unprecedented access to information and to communications; at another, it might be seen as an implement of control, giving unlimited power to those who control the information that it stores. The central dilemma of the information society is how to resolve that issue.

Studying the information society

This book has deliberately avoided a theoretical approach to the information society in favour of one which is pragmatic and empirical, grounded in the reality of the changing world of information management. It would, however, be wrong to ignore the fact that scholars in many disciplines have tried to theorize what has happened and still continues to happen. Throughout the second half of the 20th century, a succession of sociologists, historians, economists, mathematicians and computer scientists (among others!) have observed, measured, analysed and explicated the changing nature of communications and information. Many different names have been applied to the phenomena that they have studied. The economist Fritz Machlup, writing in the early 1960s, argued for the growth of a knowledge-based economy, in which extraction and manufacturing, the traditional sources of wealth in industrialized societies, would be displaced by activities which involved the discovery, processing and distribution of knowledge. His massive array of evidence was supplemented by work in the late 1970s by another political economist, Marc U. Porat, who largely confirmed Machlup's thesis. On the basis of this line of economic reasoning, Daniel Bell, an American sociologist, prophesied the coming of what he called 'the post-industrial society', in which knowledge and information underpinned a shift from an economy based on manufacturing, to one dependent on knowledge-based services. Broadly speaking, the Machlup-Bell-Porat analysis was accurate. By the beginning of the 21st century, much of world's capacity for mass manufacture of goods such as motor vehicles and computers had actually shifted from Europe and North America to east and south-east Asia. The West continues, up to a point, to provide capital and expertise, but these too are now on the move; the West is gradually becoming the customer rather than the provider, with its own economies dependent on providing value-added services, education and training, and research and development. The globalization of the world economy, facilitated by the internet and all that has come with it, is underpinned by knowledge and information rather than by coal and steel.

This essentially economic view of social change is reflected in much of the academic writing on communications and the mass media. In the early years, a mathematical approach to understanding communications was predominant, and to some extent a forerunner of the development of computing in the late 1940s. Out of the wartime work of Turing in England and Weiner and others in the USA, there developed the models which underpinned the development of computer programming and indeed the design of computers and networks. The ruthless logic which electronic computation demands could perhaps only have come from mathematicians; it was the combination of their work with that of engineers, notably at the Massachusetts Institute of Technology, which provided the basic tool of the information revolution. At the same time, however, others were studying communications and communications systems from a quite different social perspective. Sociologists in the 1960s, many arguing from the then fashionable Marxian position, saw in the evolution of the mass media a sharp break with the past. The development and application of computing in business, industry and education seemed to strengthen their case. Although the underlying theoretical framework was discredited by the end of the century, theorists such as Schiller and Habermas (who in any case repudiated his youthful Marxism) had a significant influence on how the burgeoning information society was perceived as it developed through the last two decades before the year 2000.

The scholarly discourse which emerged can be summarized (very crudely) as being a debate between those who saw the information (or post-industrial) society as something radically new – which was the basic position of Habermas and Bell, for example – and those who saw it as the end-product of evolutionary development. This was a position increasingly adopted in the 1990s especially by those who sought to apply some of these theoretical writings to contemporary politics. The theorists of the centre-left in the post-communist world (most obviously New Labour in the UK) almost ignored the concept of the information society, while recognizing the need to address the political issues which were arising from it. They were concerned with such issues as cross-media ownership (of the press and the broadcast media, for example) and with extra-territorial broadcasting, while at the same time advocating the use of new technologies in government and in education. But there was no real agreement. Manual Castells, perhaps the most acute of all the social analysts of these phenomena, certainly argues that networks have wrought fundamental change, but he takes an essentially humanistic and optimistic view of the consequences.

These are large issues. But they are part of the context in which contemporary and future information professionals have to think about their work and their profession. All analysts agree that knowledge and the information that it embodies is fundamental to human activity. Their theoretical disagreements (as opposed to their different political stances) actually coalesce around a debate about whether the transformative power of computers and networks has been so great as to be revolutionary. A reader of Chapters 1 and 2 of this book may take the view that this proposition is difficult to sustain. There is evidence that organized societies have always depended on information, and have for centuries recognized its significance. For much of the 20th century there were conscious efforts to bring the growing body of recorded human knowledge under control. The theory of information science and the practice of information management were developed largely in response to this imperative. The new tools that were provided by the development of the computer, and the subsequent linkage between computation and communication, facilitated this response but were not in themselves the cause of it. In the debate between continuity and change, it is the continuity of the problems rather than the changes in the mechanics of their solution which seems to have the balance in its favour.

A note on further reading

Like the book itself, this note is intended to give guidance to the novice rather than the specialist. There is a large and still growing literature on almost every aspect of the subject. Technological innovation is so rapid that few can follow it comprehensively in the specialist literature. Indeed, perhaps the best sources of information and interpretation are the newspapers; in Britain, both *The Guardian* and *The Independent* have regular, well informed and intelligent pages on information technology issues, and the social and political dimensions are dealt with, either directly or by implication, throughout the press and the broadcast media. The major broadsheets in the USA are similarly thorough in their coverage; indeed *The New York Times* is probably more comprehensive than any other newspaper in the world. In all serious papers, however, there is regular material, both news and features, which bears directly on the subjects covered in this book. At a slightly more specialized level, both *New Scientist* and *Scientific American* contain a great deal of relevant material. On a more considered basis the issues are also addressed by generalist writers from Alvin Toffler to Paul Kennedy. To understand such issues, there is no real substitute for a wide awareness of current events and concerns.

More specifically, two books aimed at a similar audience to this one have covered some of the same ground, and can usefully be read in conjunction with it. These are: Susan Hornby and Zoë Clarke, *Challenge and Change in the Information Society*, Facet Publishing, 2003; and James Dearnley and John Feather, *The Wired World: an introduction to the theory and practice of the information society*, Library Association Publishing, 2001. Both begin to address some of the theoretical issues which are largely avoided here, but, for a more detailed account of these, see Frank Webster, *Theories of the Information Society*, 2nd edn, Routledge, 2002. There is an historical perspective in Armand Mattelart, *Histoire de la Société de l'Information*, Editions La Découverte & Syros, 2001, translated as *The Information Society: an introduction*, Sage, 2003. Michael W. Hill, *The Impact of Information on Society*, Bowker-Saur, 1999, is also useful. A recent study of the pre-computer information society, which offers many new and valuable insights, is Alistair Black, Dave Muddiman and Helen Plant, *The Early Information Society: information management in Britain before the computer*, Ashgate, 2007.

Inevitably, in such a rapidly changing field, monographs and textbooks are soon dated, but some have a more permanent value by raising long-term issues. Such works include R. L. Katz, *The Information Society: an international perspective*, Praeger, 1988; David Lyon, *The Information Society: issues and illusions*, Polity Press, 1987; and William J. Martin, *The Information Society*, Aslib, 1988. Two classic studies, of which every student should be aware, are Fritz Machlup, *The Production and Distribution of Knowledge in the United States*, Princeton University Press, 1962; and Marc Porat, *The Information Economy: definition and measurement*, United States Department of Commerce, 1977. More recent general studies include Charles Jonscher, *The Evolution of Wired Life*, Wiley, 1999; and Wendy Currie, *The Global Information Society*, Wiley, 2000.

Further study of the historical subjects in Chapters 1 and 2 can be pursued in Elizabeth Eisenstein, *The Printing Press as an Agent of Change: communications and culture in early modern Europe*, 2 vols, Cambridge University Press, 1979; and in Adrian Johns, *The Nature of the Books: print and knowledge in the making*, University of Chicago Press, 1998. On more recent history, see Brian Winston, *Media, Technology and Society. A History: from the telegraph to the internet*, Routledge, 1998; and John Naughton, *A Brief History of the Future: the origin of the internet*, Weidenfeld & Nicolson, 1999. As its title implies, the latter is far from being entirely historical. A rare reflective insight into one of the makers of the cyber-revolution will be found in Tim Berners-Lee, *Weaving the Web: the past, present and future of the world wide web by its inventor*, Orion Business Books, 1999. For a series of perceptive essays by an acute journalistic observer of developments, see

James Gleick, *What Just Happened: a chronicle from the information frontier*, Abacus, 2002. There is a useful account of one of the giants of the early 21st century in David A. Vise, *The Google Story*, Pan, 2006.

Different forms of communication systems, such as those provided by publishers, authors, librarians and educators, are dealt with in A. J. Meadows (ed.), *Knowledge and Communication: essays on the information chain*, Library Association Publishing, 1991. On publishing, the best brief general introduction is probably Giles N. Clark, *Inside Book Publishing: a career builder's guide*, 3rd edn, Routledge, 2000, although this is a description of operations rather than a consideration of issues. On a broader canvas, the work of Philip G. Altbach, especially in *The Knowledge Context: comparative perspectives on the distribution of knowledge*, State University of New York Press, 1987, is seminal and cannot be ignored. For a recent analysis, see John Feather, *Communicating Knowledge: publishing in the 21st century*, K. G. Saur, 2003.

On political and policy issues, see Jane Steele and Nick Moore, *Information-intensive Britain: an analysis of the policy issues*, Policy Studies Institute, 1991; and Ian Miles, *Information Technology and Information Society: options for the future*, Economic and Social Research Council, 1988. For a largely American perspective on many important issues with much wider implications, see James E. Katz and Ronald E. Rice, (eds.), *Social Consequences of Internet Use: access, involvement, and interaction*, MIT Press, 2002. For a current view of legal and political issues, see the Yale Information Society Project website (http:// islandia. law.yale.edu/isp/). On the issues dealt with in Chapter 5, see Trevor Hayward, *Info-rich, Info-poor: access and exchange in the global information society*, Bowker-Saur, 1995; and Mohan Munasinghe (ed.), *Computers and Informatics in Developing Countries*, Butterworth, 1989. For a contemporary American domestic perspective, see *America in the Information Age*, the website of the Digital Divide Project (www.ntia.doc.gov/ntiahome/digitaldivide). The European dimension will be found on the European Union's website at http://europa. eu.int/information_society/index_en.htm. General and statistical data on internet access, availability and use will be found on the ClickZ Network at www.clickz.com/.

By far the most detailed study of the whole subject, however, which must be consulted by all students, is the great work by the sociologist Manuel Castells, published under the general title of *The Information Age: economy, society and culture*. The three volumes are: *The Rise of the Network Society*, Blackwell, 1996; *The Power of Identity*, Blackwell, 1997; and *End of Millennium*, Blackwell, 1998. The same author's Clarendon Lectures in Management, delivered at Oxford in 2000, give a succinct account of his position on one key aspect of the topic: Manuel Castells, *The Internet Galaxy: reflections on the internet, business, and society*, Oxford University Press, 2001. The journal *The Information Society* (1981–) is essential for serious study; for an account of it, and a list of key papers, see the current editor's historical study (www.ics.uci.edu/ukling/tishist.html). The literature teems with speculative studies on the future of the information professions. This cannot be disentangled from the future of the services they provide, so that many insights can be found in such documents as *New Library: The People's Network* (www.ukoln.ac.uk/services/lic.newlibrary/), Chapter 3. The approach of one major political and economic grouping can be studied in European Commission, *Building the European Information Society for Us All: final policy report of the high-level expert group April 1997*, Brussels, 1997.

Index